AGNES DE MILLE

DANCING OFF THE EARTH

A glamorous portrait of Agnes de Mille taken when she lived in England during the 1920s. How could she have doubted her own beauty? (Janet Jevous, London. Hearst Newspaper Collection, University of Southern California Library.)

AGNES DE MILLE

DANCING OFF THE EARTH

BEVERLY GHERMAN

Philip Weltner Library
Atlanta, Georgia

ATHENEUM   1990   NEW YORK

Atheneum
Macmillan Publishing Company
866 Third Avenue, New York, NY 10022
Collier Macmillan Canada, Inc.
First Edition
Printed in the United States of America
10   9   8   7   6   5   4   3   2   1
Library of Congress Cataloging-in-Publication Data
Gherman, Beverly.
Agnes de Mille : dancing off the earth/by Beverly Gherman
—1st ed.   p.   cm.
Bibliography: p.   Includes index.
Summary: The life and accomplishments of the choreographer, dancer, and author best known for the ballets
she created on American themes and for the choreography of the musical Oklahoma!
ISBN 0–689–31441–8
1. de Mille, Agnes—Juvenile literature. 2. Dancers—United States—Biography—Juvenile literature.
3. Choreographers—United States—Biography—Juvenile literature. [1. de Mille, Agnes. 2. Dancers.
3. Choreographers.] I. Title.
GV1785.D36G44 1990
792.8'092—dc20
[B]   [92]   89-6888   CIP   AC

Books by Beverly Gherman

Georgia O'Keeffe
THE "WIDENESS AND WONDER" OF HER WORLD

Agnes de Mille
DANCING OFF THE EARTH

TO RUTH, WHO EXPLAINED A DANCER'S SPACE;
TO CHUCK, WHO EXPLORED THE DANCER'S WORLD WITH ME;
AND TO DOTTY AND JANE, WHO KEPT SMILING THROUGH THE MANY
REVISIONS

"To dance means:
to step out on the great stages of the world . . .
to flash and soar . . .
to ride violins and trumpets . . .
to feel the magic work . . ."

—Agnes de Mille, *To a Young Dancer*

CONTENTS

ACKNOWLEDGMENTS

In the beginning, Elaine Cahn gave me her dance collection and her memories; Miles Kreuger, of the Film and Musicals Institute, shared his expertise and his video of Agnes de Mille's choreography; Ruth Lert opened her Dance Library and Archives, as well as her heart, to me.

The staffs of the Dance Collection at the New York Public Library, the Sophia Smith Collection and College Archives at Smith College, the Archives of Performing Arts at the University of Southern California, the Archives of Performing Arts in San Francisco, and the Beverly Hills Public Library made their material and their assistance available to me.

My editor, Marcia Marshall, patiently guided me through the many "visions and revisions" of the manuscript.

Thank you all.

AGNES DE MILLE

DANCING OFF THE EARTH

CHAPTER 1

IN THE SPOTLIGHT

FROM HER BOX AT NEW YORK'S METROPOLITAN OPERA HOUSE, AGNES de Mille waited for the curtain to rise on her new ballet, *The Informer.* Her posture erect and her hair swept into a tight chignon, Agnes at eighty-two still gave the appearance of the regal dancer she had been. It was May 1988, but within minutes she and the rest of the audience would be transported to the Ireland of 1916, where the dancers would spin their tragic tale set against the anguish of civil war.

From the time she was just a girl, Agnes had been able to take her audiences to other worlds through her dance stories. Sometimes the stories were light and humorous; often they were tragic and serious. Sometimes she used the emotions and events in her own life as inspiration for her stories.

Agnes with Mikhail Baryshnikov during the New York opening of *The Informer,* 1988. (Vic de Lucia. *New York Times.*)

Occasionally she chose events important to history. Always she combined the art of classical ballet with other dance styles as she created her original productions.

Agnes loved to dance and to create dances. In fact, she insisted she began to walk and to dance at almost the same moment. She hardly remembered a time when she did not dance. Even her mother recalled how in her first bath Agnes had gone "straight into the water on the points of her toes." In her early years she danced mainly for her family, especially when they lived in the country. Most evenings after supper, with the light fading and the crickets chirping in unison, Mother played favorite tunes on the piano while Agnes whirled and twirled and joyously moved her body to the music's rhythms.

One summer afternoon when she was almost six, she discovered the intoxicating taste of performing before a larger audience. Fresh from a bath, her golden red curls still damp, her body glistening with olive oil, she skipped onto the Merriewold porch to greet Aunt Bettie. Animated voices from the tennis court lured her farther from the house, and she followed the rough stone wall as it wound beneath the trees. "Stark naked," she danced along, enjoying the dappled sunshine on her body, the feel of the mossy path underfoot. Through the trees she could see Father and his friends playing tennis. All the neighbors were watching, their eyes intently following the ball as it flew across the net, from side to side. Agnes crept on, moving closer to the courts, almost daring them to notice her instead of the game.

Just as he was to serve, Father did see her. "You'll catch cold!" he called, urging her to return to the house. Agnes didn't move a muscle. Instead she stood watching until she heard them all begin to laugh, a hearty, joyful laughter. Later in life, she remembered the scene and described with relish how she eventually and very "slowly wheeled around and retreated. Dignified. Never hurried. It pleased me—that laughter—that was the wine."

Little did her first audience of family and friends realize the great impact Agnes de Mille would have on the future dance world. From the beginning, her parents were against her becoming a dancer because dance was considered a scandalous activity when Agnes was growing up in the early 1900s. The prevailing attitude was that nice girls did not become dancers. She was to change that attitude, starting right in the rooms of her own home and with those closest to her.

Eventually Agnes would bring ballet to American audiences through ballet companies and in musical comedies on stage and screen, and she would bring respect to the dancer and the art of dance. But she did not accomplish these goals overnight. She worked for many years and against many obstacles.

CHAPTER 2

LIFE AT MERRIEWOLD

SUMMERS AT MERRIEWOLD WERE ALWAYS SPECIAL FOR AGNES. AS A child she felt a great sense of freedom in the country estate that had once belonged to her grandfather, Henry George. She pranced in and out of the house, enjoying the earth under her feet. She hopped up and down the stairs, using the banister as her first barre. At home in New York City, the family lived in an apartment high above the ground, where she could only peer wistfully through the windows and long for the outdoors. She could never go out alone. She had to wait until her mother or her nurse, Mamie, was free. She had to bundle up and wait for the clanging, slow elevator, which seemed to stop at every floor. Once the bronze door unfolded to let her out, she still had to walk through the lobby and greet the doorman before at last she reached the grass in Morningside Park.

In 1905, when Agnes was born in the New York flat on 118th Street, it was considered most "modest" that her

4

mother be attended by a "lady" doctor. Several years later her sister, Margaret, was also born there, and the two sisters spent those early years always fighting head colds, always being bundled up for their walks outside, and always being reminded to act like ladies, not rowdies, inside the apartment. Their father, William de Mille, was a successful New York playwright who was also "dashing, handsome, and lean," according to Agnes. He adored his daughters but he "referred to us for the first eight years of our lives as 'the boys.' . . . 'How are my fellers?' he wrote Mother. . . . 'How are the boys doing? Kiss my boys good-night.' " Agnes laughed about this in later life, but perhaps this is when she first became convinced she could accomplish whatever she wanted; as her father's "feller," she would not be limited by the constraints other young women had to face in the early 1900s.

William's father had left the ministry to become a playwright, but on his deathbed he pleaded with his wife, Bernice, to keep their two sons away from the theater. He wanted William and Cecil to have fine educations and secure professions; engineering seemed like an excellent choice. In order to support herself and the boys, the widowed Bernice found it necessary to open a school for children. She even saw to it that William and Cecil graduated with engineering degrees. But she could not keep them from turning eventually to their first love, the theater.

As a playwright, William worked closely with his stars and encouraged them to visit often for "teas or evening receptions." Agnes grew up surrounded by beautiful women moving through the de Mille drawing room. She was enchanted by their smiling glances, the graceful way they walked in long, fitted dresses, their tiny waists corseted, their heads held high under broad-brimmed hats. She pictured herself becoming an actress—walking, talking, and smiling before her own approving audience.

In the meantime, Agnes lived for the summers when the family left New York City to travel six long hours to Merriewold. They took three different trains and a ferry, arriving at St. Joseph Station in the southeast corner of New York State. Frank Felter was always waiting for them with a wagon and two farm horses to drive them the last three miles up to the house. Frank did everything around the place, including cleaning game animals or the fish Father caught. Agnes stooped right next to Frank, watching every move as he gutted and disposed of the hare's entrails or the trout's fins. She also sat next to him on the wagon seat so that she could inform Margaret and her parents when either of the horses left large, steamy droppings.

As soon as they arrived at the house, Agnes rushed inside to discover the small creatures that had lived or died there during the winter. She might find baby mice in the pantry or possums in the nursery or a skunk family in the cellar. Instead of feeling dismayed, Agnes was curious about everything. It didn't matter to her that the house smelled musty and damp for days after they arrived. Mother would eventually air it out by keeping all the windows and doors open.

At Merriewold, Agnes was in touch with all her senses, especially with the way the earth felt under her feet, the minute she stepped out the front door. Many years later she found the words to describe that feeling when she wrote in a history of dance how American Indians touched the earth through their glove-soft moccasins: "The foot felt the earth, caressed it, made love to it—the whole foot."

CHAPTER 3

IN THE WOODS

EARLY-MORNING SOUNDS WOKE AGNES IN THE COUNTRY. FROM BE-
neath her mosquito netting, she heard the chatter of birds
and the creaking iron roller Frank used to flatten the clay of
the tennis court. Dressing quickly, she raced downstairs to
gobble up her oatmeal and freshly picked huckleberries. Her
imaginary pals were waiting—Gockle in the sunflower patch
or Dickie on a special boulder under the trees.

Agnes spent the morning with those friends, listening to
forest sounds and smelling the perfume of the pine trees.
She whirled under the ancient rhododendrons or made mud
pies beneath the pink canopy of blossoming mountain lau-
rels until it was time for swimming.

At eleven o'clock, she and Margaret walked with Mother
to the lake, where they joined their aunts and cousins inside
damp, wooden dressing rooms. All the young children
changed into bathing outfits quite openly in front of each

other. Agnes couldn't resist peeking at the spectacle of the older girls and their mothers struggling into woolen serge suits while modestly trying to keep themselves covered.

Swimming lessons were serious business to Mother. For Agnes, the best time came after the lessons were finished, when she was able to romp in the cool water, fighting its resistance against her body. At the very last moment, she took her turn on the rope swing hanging from the branch of an old maple tree. How exhilarating it was to fly through the air, high above the water. In later years, she must have experienced that same joy every time she leaped into the air, or "danced off the earth," in ballet performances.

At Merriewold, Father spent his mornings writing plays in a small cabin in the woods, and no one was allowed to make noise or to disturb him until the family came together for a large meal at one o'clock.

During that midday meal, Mother, looking radiant, sat at one end of the table. Agnes was sure she was the most beautiful mother of all. No one else had such lovely golden red hair, such brilliant blue eyes, or such dainty size-one feet. She was also very smart and very much a perfectionist. Her father had been Henry George, the great nineteenth-century philosopher and economist.

Anna de Mille diligently carried on his single-tax concept throughout her life, firmly believing, as he had, that the government should levy only one tax and that tax should be based on the value of land. She attended to her husband and daughters, stitched their clothes, supported their every endeavor, and maintained her handsome English gardens. She also found time to work on her father's biography and recruit new believers for his ideas; in later years, even Agnes's dancers were enlisted in her classes.

Anna and William de Mille, Agnes's parents, before a bust of Henry George, Agnes's grandfather. (Photographer unknown. William de Mille Collection, Archives of Performing Arts, University of Southern California.)

Anna and the other mothers visited together on Merriewold porches in the afternoons, embroidering or making delicate lace while they listened to poetry. Agnes, comfortably settled under the oaks, "stringing phlox blossoms on long grasses," would drop everything and run as soon as she heard the butcher's wagon wheels or the bell on the vegetable man's wagon. She hung over the sides, watching Mother select choice cuts of meat or freshly picked corn and carrots, while trying not to bump into the many strips of flypaper covered with tiny corpses.

The family's food was cooled in a small icebox, by ice chunks that Frank had packed in sawdust during the winter. Everything was made by hand: Ice cream was turned with salt and ice chips until it reached the right consistency; mayonnaise was whipped by a "strong arm" and even then might take "an hour of beating." Mother spent long mornings cooking fruit jams over the wood-burning stove. The de Milles were fortunate to have running water inside their house, but they still had to use chamber pots or the communal outhouse.

Mother never sat with idle hands and never allowed the children to do so either. Agnes was taught to sew when she was only three, beginning with hems, seams, and buttonholes and graduating to cross-stitch and embroidery.

Their only quiet time was in the evenings after a light supper. Agnes and Margaret, in their cozy, long nighties, would settle in front of the fire, and Pop would light the oil lamp and read to them from *Uncle Remus* or Kipling's *Just So Stories.* He always managed to turn it into a performance with his deep, dramatic voice and the proper dialect. Not wanting to waste a single opportunity for improvement, Mother made sure the girls said their nightly prayers in French before they went to sleep.

Sometimes Agnes heard Father singing, while Mother or Aunt Bettie played the piano for him. She insisted on taking piano lessons, thinking that in a few weeks she would be able to accompany him, but once she began lessons she discovered that it might take a little longer, perhaps years, before she would be good enough. Her teacher, Edward Meyerhofer, was very strict and made her learn how to count and practice Czerny exercises for twenty minutes every day. Sometimes she hid behind the sofa or bookcase to avoid practicing, and Mother had to drag her out. Agnes wanted to play real music, she told Mr. Meyerhofer, not always scales and exercises. Finally he gave her "Brownies in the Rain," and she was satisfied for the time being. It was not until she had practiced diligently, two hours a day, for many years, that she was eventually able to play music written by Schumann, Chopin, and Liszt, and all the songs Father loved to sing.

Most of the time Agnes enjoyed her younger sister's antics, but sometimes she was not happy having Margaret follow her all around. Once she grew so angry she choked Margaret and acted quite smug about it until Mother put both of her dainty hands around Agnes's throat and let her know what it felt like to be choked. It gave Agnes quite a shock, and she never did it again. After that, Agnes found the best way to deal with Margaret was to ignore her. She played with Gockle and Dickie, danced about the house or under the trees, and pretended Margaret did not exist at all.

Late in life she insisted, "I always was most alive in the woods. My hair got redder. I moved directly, like an animal. I was quiet, I listened. I knew about waiting. I liked waiting. I relished it."

CHAPTER 4

WEST TO CALIFORNIA

YEAR AFTER YEAR AGNES HEARD WHAT A SUCCESS FATHER'S LATEST play had been. In his dramas he told stories about families and interpersonal relationships, with great awareness of social problems. He seemed to know exactly what the public wanted to see. Then one year he wrote a play that failed, and he was ready to try something new.

When his brother, Cecil, brought his first silent film, *The Squaw Man,* to New York, William was thrilled by its possibilities. "I saw unrolled before my eyes the first really new form of dramatic storytelling which had been invented for some 500 years." He was moved by the story, even though the film kept breaking and the musical accompaniment didn't suit the story at all.

In 1913, when Cecil had moved to the small, sleepy "village of orange groves and pepper trees" called Hollywood to make motion pictures for the new industry, he kept urging

William to join him, to turn his writing talents from the stage to silent films. Until then, William had refused, calling the films "galloping tintypes" and insisting he would never give up writing for the stage. Now he agreed to give motion pictures a try, but only for a few months.

Early silent films were often jerky productions. Camera techniques had not been perfected, and the results were blurred black-and-white scenes followed by printed sentences to explain what the actors were saying or doing. Gestures were often exaggerated to make up for lack of sound, and symphonic music was often added to heighten the dramatic effect of the on-screen action. In a love scene, the couple's lips might be proclaiming their passion, mouths and arms moving at a rapid clip, while the audience heard only a medley of serenading violins. In a Western, galloping horses on the villain's trail would be accompanied by an orchestra's rising crescendo. Often there was an organ accompaniment in the theater when the film was shown.

William found he loved the outdoor life and the challenges of filmmaking. In less than six weeks he wrote to Anna to close up the apartment and bring Agnes and Margaret out to California. Anna was thrilled. She thought moving would be an adventure, and moving to California would mean warm weather and fewer colds for Agnes and Margaret. Agnes did not want to move. She wept over leaving Merriewold and tried to memorize everything within the house: "the graining of the wood in our nursery, the arrangement of dishes on the shelves downstairs, the warp of the kitchen floor." She knew she would never forget the magical forest with its flowers and freedom.

Agnes was also very worried over what she would find in California. She heard there would be tall, pointed mountains everywhere. How ever would they be able to hang onto such mountains? Then she heard that it never rained in California during the summer. How would anything grow without rain? Worst of all, Mamie would not be moving to California with them. How would she manage without her beloved Mamie?

Well, maybe life would not be a total disaster if she could have her own horse to ride, be lucky enough to go to school with an Indian boy, and of course, become an actress in the movies.

Traveling by train from the East to the West, Agnes watched the landscape change from urban towns with homes tightly packed together to broad prairie lands surrounding very few homes. The vast space made a special impression on her and eventually would reappear in her first ballet choreography when she began to produce dances with uniquely American themes. "The memory waited like a hunger for all my life to make itself known at the sympathetic time."

As soon as they arrived in California, Mother found them a "dear little ugly house" to rent, with a blooming rose garden and an exotic banana tree. The owner was an elderly lady who discovered William was part of the motion picture industry and quickly changed her mind. "A movie! . . . I couldn't possibly rent my house to a movie," she kept insisting. They eventually convinced her they were reliable people, the girls were "two little angels," and they would all take good care of her house.

As they explored Hollywood, Agnes realized it was just another small town similar to those in the East, but here the streets were lined with shaggy palm trees rather than stately maples and chestnuts. Sadly she realized she would not be riding trails on her own horse and there would be no Indian children in her school. Instead Mother had found the Hollywood School for Girls, where classes met under the trees unless it rained (and it certainly did rain in California, in the winter and the spring). Agnes made friends with many movie children, and she met Mary Hunter, who would become a lifelong friend.

In the distance, Agnes could see the mountains—they were really hills—surrounding the town. Those same hills would someday be the setting for enormous white metal letters spelling out HOLLYWOOD, almost as an early advertisement for the film capital it was to become. Rather than fearing them, how Agnes came to love those hills! She wanted to run down them, roll along their grassy slopes, feel the earth against her body. "They hurt me, those hills. I loved them so." When she was eleven she described those hills in her diary as the "most wonderful thing I've ever seen. The mountains on each side of you, the desert before you. The mountains beyond the desert are pinks and grey and browns. The desert itself is grey with great patches of grey shadow here and there."

CHAPTER 5

MOVING PICTURES

THE FAMILY QUICKLY SETTLED INTO THEIR NEW LIFE IN HOLLYWOOD, with movies becoming important to all of them. Uncle Cecil's first film, *The Squaw Man,* turned out to be a huge success. Using an old barn, with stables for his stars' dressing rooms, he and his partners learned and perfected techniques of filming as they went along.

William brought his own changes to the studio. Before he arrived, stories were discussed at meetings and the action improvised during filming. He insisted that each plot be written out ahead of time as he had done for the stage. He formed a scenario department and hired an assistant to write the stories with him. In his memoirs, William described how "we thought pictures, ate pictures, dreamed pictures" especially in the beginning years.

Mother occasionally called the school principal to excuse Agnes and Margaret from school for the day because Cecil

16

"was throwing Gloria Swanson to the lions" or burning Joan of Arc at the stake. Dressed alike in their middy blouses and straw hats, the sisters would get their education that day watching the filming of one of Uncle Cecil's grand film spectacles. While Cecil worried about getting each detail perfect, Agnes found herself "transfixed" by the dramatic scenes being enacted before her. She became the heroine, spoke her lines, wept her tears, and suffered her pain. On the set of *Joan of Arc*, Agnes watched as Joan, played by Geraldine Farrar, was dressed in armor and lifted onto a handsome white stallion. Uncle Cecil explained the scene to the large group of actors and then called for the take. Joan dramatically led the French in a charge across the fields to fight and defeat the English in the battle of Orléans. That night Agnes wrote in her diary, "It was the most beautiful scene I've ever seen and one of the most wonderful I ever shall see."

Several days later Agnes watched them burn Joan at the stake. She saw the flames leap up the young girl, her body writhing, her arms and head overcome with fire, her hair ablaze. Agnes began to perspire, her throat felt dry, her eyes watered. The air grew hazy, and she could not shut out the smell of fire. It enveloped her. She had to keep reminding herself it was not really Joan they were burning, that it was only a dummy going up in smoke. After watching the emotional scene, Agnes was glad to return home, where she could climb up in her favorite tree and read quietly by herself. After the film was completed, Uncle Cecil gave her a sword, arrows, and spear points from the set, mementos Agnes treasured and used for the castle she was building.

Sometimes Agnes did not like the films she saw and complained in her diary, "Father is taking *Anton the Terrible*. That's all the picture is—tortures." Watching an actor being beaten until his back spurted blood, she wrote, "It nearly made me sick. . . . Everything got blurred. I could hardly see. My eyes acked [sic]. The people became dim figures moving all around." She felt the same sadness when she saw a dog get run over and wept at its agony, or many years later when she attended a bullfight. She could not watch the animal being tortured and was sickened by "the cheers and applause and laughter that come from the audience after each blow dealt the bewildered animal." She even likened the audience's reaction to the response in the theater "when they do not realize that the thing that they are looking at is not comedy but tragedy."

Agnes described her feelings in her diaries from the time she was very young until she was twenty. She used ruled pages, to which she added the date. Sometimes she wrote with fountain pen; sometimes she used pencil. She listed all her activities and even the books she read.

When she was ten, Agnes played her first screen role in the first film her father directed, *The Ragamuffin.* She took her part seriously, studying in a mirror the facial expressions she would need to look like the young waif she played. There were lines to learn even though it was a silent film, and often she had to cry. She told her diary how she practiced weeping and "succeeded in getting one tear in my right eye."

When she was not performing in a movie, she and her friend Luiginia spent hours working on their costume books, cutting out pictures of exotic outfits or drawing original ideas. Agnes made place cards for the guests invited to Mother's parties, designing each one as if it were an original work of art.

Agnes at age eleven. (Rosher. Dance Collection, the New York Public Library.)

The girls loved to dress up and hike to their clubhouse in the hills, picking wildflowers as they went along, the dog Pepper following them on the trail and stopping to sniff at every bush. Agnes was also studying French that summer, taking music lessons, and learning how to crochet.

If she ever found a moment to herself, Agnes climbed up in her favorite tree and read from *Master Skylark* or *The Lass of the Silver Sword.* Her friends knew she loved to read, and on her eleventh birthday most of them brought her books or pictures. Father gave her a set of Louisa May Alcott's stories, and Margaret, costumes for her costume book. Uncle Cecil always remembered her with a glamorous gift of scent or lingerie. In those years she signed her name "Agnes George de Mille" and dreamed about seeing it written out on theater marquees and playbills when she became a great actress.

CHAPTER 6

DANCE PAGEANTS

MOTHER MADE SURE HER DAUGHTERS MET CULTURED PEOPLE AT HOME
and often took them to concerts or readings being given by
visiting artists. When she and Agnes went to a matinee
performance of the ballet dancer Adeline Genée, Anna had
no idea what a lasting effect it would have on her young
daughter. Leaving the theater, Agnes insisted her mother
"arrange about lessons for the next day." She now knew
what she really wanted to be—a dancer, not an actress.
Mother smiled, but no dancing lessons were provided.

Agnes begged her parents to let her take dance lessons.
They would not hear of it. After all, dancers came from a
different social class. The young dancer Ruth St. Denis was
warned by her school principal that " 'dance was a product
of the devil. I would rather see you throw yourself in the
river and drown than dance on stage.' " Agnes's father was
not quite so violent. He did think of dance as "exhibition-

21

istic acrobatics," not an "intellectual or spiritual challenge." In William's mind, dancers were on a par with prostitutes or courtesans, rather than artists. Father wanted her to become a tennis champion. "He wanted me to learn fencing and boxing. He took me fishing. He taught me photography. Above all, he wanted me to write plays." Mother agreed with Father. " 'You see,' she said. 'Your father knows you will be accepted anywhere if you play fine tennis.' "

Besides, Mother thought Agnes had an innate ability for dancing that lessons would only destroy. Agnes should enjoy her dancing but find something else to do with her life.

One afternoon in August, Mother invited Ruth St. Denis to tea. Agnes knew what a great dancer she was and began to tremble when Mother suggested Agnes perform for their guest. She finally found her courage and showed Miss St. Denis several of her dances. Before Agnes was through, Miss St. Denis kicked off her shoes and demonstrated several of her sensuous Indian and Egyptian dances, inspiring Agnes even more. In her diary she wrote, "Miss St. Denis said I had talent and that I must go to her school next year. . . . the lady who was with her said I made her cry because it was so beautiful. Wether [sic] she meant it or whether she just said it to flatter me I don't know."

Her parents would not be moved. They continued to ignore Agnes's requests for lessons. It never occurred to Agnes to disobey her parents. If Father told her to read a certain book, she read it. If he told her not to read something, she would not touch it. When both Mother and Father insisted that dancing was not something a young girl should study, she had no choice but to listen, although she secretly envied Margaret's spunk to do exactly what she wanted.

Mother did allow Agnes to take pantomime classes at school, where she learned to act out a story using gestures, and she encouraged Agnes and her friends to build a stage in the garage out of "boxes, crates, sawed-off palm branches, and old furniture." Agnes led them through all kinds of productions on that stage. Sometimes it was a castle, other times it was an inn. Always it served Agnes as a setting for her inventive mind.

Caught up by Adeline Genée's ballet performance, Agnes decided that she and her friends would give a pageant even though none of them had ever had a dance lesson. She quickly took charge, listing all the dances they would perform, improvising the steps, planning the price of tickets, and telling Mother which costumes they would need. Mother didn't object. Maybe she thought dancing on the lawn in the backyard was harmless enough. She even agreed to assist, setting out to borrow clothing and props from the neighbors while the girls spent the next week rehearsing the steps of their dances.

With her usual optimism, Agnes expected brisk ticket sales to help her support two French war orphans. She planned to charge ten or fifteen cents for each seat and assumed all the seats would be sold. The pageant was held under the banana tree, with a large audience of relatives and friends sitting in the shade of the house. Agnes was correct about the size of the audience, even though she miscalculated how great her earnings would be.

Agnes put herself first on the program. Out she swept, in a colorful Italian dress Luiginia had loaned her, with an enormous wreath of poppies and straw on her head. She danced a lively Polish polka and beamed at the audience's applause before running to change for the next dance. Later she danced a solo mostly on her toes, or *en pointe,* as the dancers called it. It was painful, because she was not wearing blocked toe shoes, but the thick grass and her strong determination made it bearable.

As each of the dances followed, she tried to perform with a smile on her face, but Aunt Mildred, who was in charge of the Victrola, played minuet music for the geisha dance, or Indian music for the minuet, and Agnes and the others grew frantic, signaling her to change. The shepherds came out looking very authentic wrapped in deerskin rugs, also provided by Aunt Mildred, and they managed to perform without any mishaps.

Just as Agnes was beginning to relax and enjoy everything, a friend began the sea nymph dance. The girl looked very beautiful in her costume, but she hardly knew the steps to her dance, and Agnes was furious. She grew even angrier when she heard the audience clap and cheer as the dance ended, because she knew it was the girl's looks that had impressed them, not her dancing. "It was the first time I had run up against biology in my professional life and I found it unreasonable," she wrote in a memoir many years later.

At school, whenever she could, Agnes peeked in to see what the dance classes were doing. She envied the girls whose parents allowed them to take those lessons and realized that not everyone agreed with her mother and father. She read everything she could find about dancing and cut out every photograph of dancers to paste in her scrapbook. She continued to beg her parents to let her take dancing lessons, and they continued to say no.

CHAPTER 7

BALLET LESSONS

Philip Weltner Library
Atlanta, Georgia

AT LAST, WHEN AGNES WAS THIRTEEN, THE DOCTOR RECOMMENDED
dance lessons for Margaret's fallen arches, and their parents
finally allowed both girls to begin lessons at Theodore Kosloff's School of Imperial Russian Ballet. Agnes wrote in her
diary that Mr. Kosloff said she had " 'no juice' " in her heels,
that her "muscles were dry, stubborn, and unresilient." He
also told her that she was too old, at thirteen, to begin
dancing. But he thought she was wonderful at pantomime,
she confided to her diary. And she also kept track of every
time Kosloff's assistant, Miss Fredova, said, " 'Very good.' "
All three times.

Agnes finally had her wish. She was taking ballet lessons.
But she very quickly discovered that she did not have an
"ideal ballet body—long limbs and a small, compact torso."
Instead she was "all rusty wire and safety pins." The ideal
foot has a high instep and an Achilles tendon with great

spring. Agnes did not have the perfect instep or the perfect tendon. But she was a strong jumper and could keep going longer than most. She also realized she could develop strong shin muscles to make up for absent heel muscles.

As hard as she worked, she felt she continued to be the worst dancer in the class. She was determined to improve, and although her parents allowed only one class lesson and one private lesson a week, she practiced diligently every day at home in Mother's bathroom. She wanted to be with the other students, practicing in the studio, but Mother felt she needed to concentrate on her schoolwork and not her dancing.

Just as ballet teachers had done for hundreds of years, Miss Fredova began every class by clapping her hands and calling the students to line up at the barre. Holding on with one hand, they moved their feet into first position, or second or third, as she directed them. In her accented French, she reminded them to keep their heads up, backs straight, knees bent. Over and over they repeated the exercises, which were based on the five classic positions named by Beauchamp, the dancing master to French king Louis XIV in the 1660s.

Then they practiced exercises for their arms, over and over, until they were dripping with perspiration. At last Miss Fredova led them to the center of the room to work on their jumps and turns and spins, always reminding them to keep their necks long, their hands graceful.

Slowly and over a long period of time, the young dancers were able to rotate their hips outward so that their heels would come together. It was not a natural movement for the body, but had developed from the movements of swordsmen who needed to race forward and backward quickly without losing their balance. When their feet and legs grew strong enough, the young women were finally allowed to put on toe shoes and to dance *en pointe,* while the young men began to practice the leaps and lifts that would be their special accomplishments.

When Agnes was fourteen, Mother took her to a Thursday-afternoon matinee to see the world-famous prima ballerina Anna Pavlova dance. Agnes and Margaret wore identical outfits of dark blue silk taffeta with matching blue hats. They reached their balcony seats at the Mason Opera House twenty minutes early, a record for Mother, who was always late because she tried to squeeze too many activities into too short a time. While they waited, Agnes studied the room's ornate ceiling and the excited audience around her. As soon as the curtain rose, her eyes were riveted on the slim, graceful Pavlova.

A few years earlier, Agnes had seen Pavlova dance, but that was before she herself became a student of ballet. Now she watched with rapt attention Pavlova's every flutter, every leap, every facial expression, hoping to capture them for her own. She could not believe how long Pavlova was able to dance *en pointe.* If only she could memorize each movement and take it home with her. She felt as though she were all alone in the theater, that Pavlova was dancing just for her. "I sat with blood beating in my throat." She was only fourteen, but now she was certain she had found her "life's work."

After the performance a friend took the three of them backstage. Agnes could hardly breathe as they climbed stairs and skirted scenery on their way. She was actually going to meet Pavlova! When they reached her dressing room, Pavlova's voice responded to their knock, and they were ushered into the presence of the famous dancer. There she stood, still dressed in a Russian peasant costume from the performance. "She spoke in light, twittering sounds, and her enormous dark eyes flashed incessantly with alertness. Her clawlike hands played nervously with the pearls at her throat." Agnes's unsteady legs would barely hold her up, and her thumping heart seemed to fill the room. Pavlova's long fingers reached out to grasp her hand and to present her with a delicate pink bouquet. When Agnes thought she could stand no more, Pavlova leaned down and kissed her.

"Anna Pavlova kissed me," she said, weeping. Margaret thought Agnes was silly and couldn't understand what there was to cry about. When they got home, Agnes, still dressed in her lovely outfit, threw herself on the ground under the trees. She lay there, reliving every moment of the afternoon and vowing to become a great dancer. For many years she treasured that small bunch of dried flowers and the memory of Pavlova's kiss. And she dreamed that Pavlova would one day notice her dancing and say, " 'That girl has talent.' "

Pavlova portraying the dying swan from *Swan Lake.* (Photographer unknown. Dance Collection, the New York Public Library.)

CHAPTER 8

GROWING UP UGLY

AGNES HAD BEEN A PRETTY CHILD WITH A SMALL BUTTON NOSE, FAIR skin, and a graceful, lithe body. She never dreamed that her looks would become a problem, but at fifteen she looked at herself in the mirror and saw a "heavy, deep-bosomed, large-hipped" young woman whose skin was muddy, whose nose was enormous, and whose teeth were crooked. She knew that by Hollywood standards, beautiful women were supposed to have delicate features, slim bodies, and flat chests.

Uncle Cecil had helped to establish those standards. To him, women should look and act like glamorous, painted dolls. And he was very outspoken in telling Agnes she "was too ugly to put a camera on." That did it. "I gave up caring how I looked—or thought I did. Except in costume," she wrote in her memoirs many years later. From the beginning she insisted on perfection in the costumes she wore for her

29

performances, yet the rest of the time she walked around in messy outfits, with disheveled hair and torn stockings.

She was oblivious to how attractive she looked when she combed her wavy hair and neatened her dress. Her expressive blue eyes and lovely complexion were evident in all her later photographs, yet Agnes saw only her defects.

To add further pain, Agnes kept comparing herself to "dainty and appealing" Margaret, who seemed more beautiful each day and was always surrounded by adoring young men. Agnes became her younger sister's chaperone, but that role did not help her learn how to charm her male classmates. Mother described her as "a moody girl, sullen in the parlor and mean in school. [She said that Agnes] entered any social gathering on the defensive with the expression 'I dare you to like me.' "

Agnes invited young men to play tennis on their private court, only to "beat the hell out of them and then dismiss them." At parties and cotillions, she found conversation with boys her age difficult and dancing even more impossible, since she had her own ideas about the steps and the pace.

The family had moved into a large Hollywood home surrounded by five acres of land, which Mother gradually transformed into exquisite English gardens. Visitors came to admire her huge beds of white iris, agapanthus, and lavender, and their blooms provided floral arrangements for many nearby churches. In springtime, blossoming apple, quince, and cherry trees turned the area into an exquisite fairyland dotted with colorful primrose, amaryllis, and fragrant nar-

Agnes arranging flowers from Mother's garden. (The Northland Studios. Hearst Newspaper Collection, University of Southern California Library.)

cissus. The spell was broken only by the barking of seven wirehaired fox terriers running about the grounds and often underfoot during tennis matches.

The de Mille house was filled with fascinating guests. One of Agnes's favorites was the great actor and comedian Charlie Chaplin, who not only performed imitations and skits for the family, but watched her performances with undivided attention. British writers W. Somerset Maugham, Rebecca West, and many others joined musicians, actors, and Mother's single taxers for tea or for Sunday supper and films.

All through high school Agnes studied ballet at Kosloff's studio and continued to practice by herself in Mother's bathroom. Agnes worked hard on her pliés, on her fouettés, her entrechats, but she found it a lonely, unrewarding existence without any encouragement from her parents and with no obvious improvement in her ability. She began to dread practice sessions and look for any excuse to avoid them.

No matter what she did the summer after graduation from high school, she found herself thinking about her future. In the middle of playing an étude on the piano or reading a poem or studying her French vocabulary, Agnes found herself worrying about her plans. If she continued to dance, where would she find a ballet group in which to perform? What would her parents think? Father had never forbidden her to dance, but she knew his feelings. Was she even good enough to consider a dancing career?

She had never received any real encouragement from anyone unless she counted the time Mr. Kosloff had introduced her as his best pantomimist or Miss St. Denis had told her she had talent. Yet she dreamed of becoming a great dancer, a Pavlova, with her name up in lights and rave reviews in every newspaper.

Agnes spent the whole vacation trying to make a decision that would please everyone. At last she knew what she would do. She walked into Father's bedroom one morning toward the end of the summer to tell him. He was standing before the mirror, shaving, his face covered with creamy lather. Agnes watched him for a few moments. " 'Pop,' " she said, " 'I've decided to give up dancing and go to college.' " Father kept his eyes riveted on the mirror as he drew the blade down his face, but Agnes saw the great relief in his eyes.

Shortly after that Agnes entered the University of California, less than a mile away from home. She had hoped to attend Mills College, a women's school in northern California, but Mother said no. It was too far away. Although Agnes continued to live at home, she was determined to have an independent life while on campus. No longer would Mother tell her exactly what to wear, what to eat, or what to read. That freshman year she had a hot dog and chocolate cake for lunch every single day. And for the first time she began to read newspapers, always forbidden to her because their pages were filled with stories about murders, rapes, and kidnappings. She even put her hair up and wore lipstick. But Mother refused to sign a form that would allow her to enroll in a required sex hygiene course.

Agnes poured all her energy into studying and found her classes as exciting as she had previously found dancing. She wanted to learn about everything and always signed up for more classes than was recommended. She was sure she knew how to write well because in high school she had been the editor of the paper, *Pine Points.* She confidently turned in her first English paper to the professor, Dr. Lily Bess Campbell, an attractive, redheaded Texan. Agnes was stunned when it was returned with a C−. Dr. Campbell told Agnes she had much to learn, and the first thing was not to take herself so seriously.

Agnes formed what would become a lifelong relationship with Dr. Campbell and got along well with the rest of the faculty. She did not do as well with her classmates. No young man even asked her out on a date that first year. Trying to ignore her isolation, she wrapped herself in a voluminous gray cape and wore a tricorne on her head, just as her mother always did. She still read and studied outside. Now she stayed underneath the trees, rather than in them. For Agnes, the most soothing locations on the campus or at home were near lush flower beds with their chorus of bees and colorful butterflies.

During her second year at UCLA, things began to change. She heard there was to be a benefit for Berkeley students whose dormitory had burned in a campus fire. She knew she had to participate. It would be her first time on a real stage, but in her dreams she had been performing ever since she saw Adeline Genée and Pavlova dance.

From the moment she set foot on stage, Agnes knew she belonged there. She performed several French sketches for the appreciative audience. It felt wonderful to be dancing again, and suddenly everyone noticed her. Sororities clamored for her to join. She quickly made friends. Dr. Campbell kept warning her that she did not have a dancer's body, that she should write; if she insisted on performing, at least she should act. Agnes ignored the advice and thought of new dances she and her friends could perform for future rallies.

She had to resume practicing and doing exercises in order

Agnes and friends performing in a campus recital, 1924. (Photographer unknown. Hearst Special Collections, University of Southern California Library.)

to get her body back in shape. Late at night after hours of studying, she put on her ballet shoes and tried to work as quietly as possible in order not to wake the family. But one night her father came out of his study and found her twirling down the hall. " 'All this education and I'm still just the father of a circus,' " he complained.

CHAPTER 9

DANCING AGAIN

AGNES WOULD HAVE LIKED HER FATHER'S APPROVAL AS SHE RESUMED
dancing, but now she was finding great personal satisfaction
in performing and in the acceptance of her classmates.

When an actor friend of Margaret's, Douglass Montgomery, saw Agnes dance, he was so moved he insisted she
forget about her education and get into the theater. " 'You're
a great dancer,' " he told her, with tears in his eyes. No one
had ever given her a compliment like that before, and it was
just what she needed to hear. It was late, but not too late,
for her to return to the dancing she had always loved.

Agnes received her university degree with honors from
UCLA in June 1926. She had studied astronomy, paleon-
tology, and poetry, and had finally taken the required course
in sex hygiene because the university insisted. She had read
the classics and written long, original papers critiquing
them. Yet deep within her, she knew she still wanted to
dance.

The day after graduation, her parents came to her and explained they were going to end their twenty-three-year marriage. Agnes adored both of her parents, and it was a terrible blow to learn that Father wanted to leave her mother. She remembered the many nights they had stolen away without her to go boating on the Merriewold lake and how they had walked together through the trees, listening for the special song of the wood thrush and searching for lilies of the valley. She had always associated their love with Merriewold, and it was doubly hurting when Father gave her the Merriewold house as part of the separation. To show support for her mother, she decided to break off all contact with her father. It would be two long years before she saw him again.

Mother took Agnes and Margaret to Europe that summer, but Anna was in a state of shock over the divorce and could think of nothing else. Even the sights and sounds of new countries would not be able to distract Anna or lift her depression.

Aboard ship Agnes composed poems, visualized dances, and wrote letters to her friends at home. Once the three of them arrived in England, they toured the Tower of London and Westminster Abbey, and Agnes filled her diary with details and sketches of those sights and of each castle and monument they saw. Poetically she described the Eiffel Tower as "a bow for a giant musical instrument strung together with nervous vibrant wires." It also reminded her of "the spring and energy in a dancer's foot."

As much as Agnes enjoyed visiting London and Paris, there was an undercurrent of sadness every time she looked at Mother. On the return trip, she could no longer avoid thinking about the changes to come in their lives. They would be leaving their beautiful Hollywood home, with its gardens and hills and the many friends they had known. They would be moving back to a glamorous New York City, but without Father. It was the end of summer and the end of a familiar and comfortable life.

Mother forced herself and Agnes into action as soon as they were on land. In just a few days, she had found an apartment in New York and Agnes had enrolled in a school of dance.

Dug Montgomery was also in town, appearing in a play. He spent a great deal of his free time with Agnes, still encouraging her to dance. In fact, he suggested she give a New York concert. Agnes thought it was a splendid idea. She would let the New York world know she existed. First she had to plan a program, and that was something she had been doing since her early pageants. Yet most of those dances were based on what she had seen Pavlova or St. Denis perform on stage.

For her first concert she wanted to present original dances—dances that would express the emotions she was feeling. She could not shake her sadness about her parents' divorce and her own insecurity about what she was doing. Being in Europe had given her some distance to look at her own country and to miss its people and its youthful energy.

With all of these thoughts and the ideas she had had on the ship, Agnes began to develop new dances. *Stagefright,* one of the first, was based on dancers she had seen in the work of French artist Edgar Degas, who had spent a great deal of his time behind the scenes at a Paris ballet studio, drawing and sculpting the dancers in action.

In the dance she called *'49,* Agnes told the story of the gold rush. Dressed in a long calico dress and with a sunbonnet on her head, she used steps from folk and popular Amer-

Agnes studying a Degas sculpture of a ballerina. (Photographer unknown. Dance Collection, the New York Public Library.)

ican music to capture the adventurous pioneer spirit of that time. She had a strong sense of patriotism and a passion about the country that had begun when she had first traveled across country by train at the age of nine.

Agnes created five or six studies based on Degas's dancers. At last, in *Ballet Class,* she created a dance in honor of the small Degas sculpture she had seen at the Metropolitan Museum of Art. The dancer, who seems exhausted yet satisfied after many hours of practice, always reminded Agnes of herself. Looking at the statuette she could almost feel its "aching knees, the strained back, the dirty smudged face, the pride."

For the dance, Agnes used the setting of the practice room in which she and the other students began their exercises at the barre with pliés. She wanted to show the audience how dancers stretch every part of their body to warm up their muscles and limbs, how they repeat the positions of their feet and arms over and over again, just as a pianist continues to play scales on the piano.

In all her dances, Agnes was communicating ideas or emotions she had experienced. She was acting out a story, using gestures as well as dance. Kosloff had been right. She was an excellent pantomimist, and she had an instinctive sense of comedic timing.

Dug attended her many rehearsals, usually after the curtain went down on his play. He approved or criticized every move. He insisted Agnes make each gesture meaningful, just as he had learned to do in his acting.

Mother was there, too. She had become Agnes's staunch supporter, emotionally and physically. She worked on every costume, made calls to friends to buy tickets, took care of every detail. She had not given up her devotion to the single taxers, but she transferred her support from William to Agnes and no longer questioned Agnes's choice of career.

Agnes approached the first concert with a great sense of self-confidence. There was no doubt in her mind that she would do well and that she would be appreciated. She was right on both scores, and the reviews were excellent. One critic wrote that she "showed herself an instinctive artist from the moment she appeared before the footlights." Agnes assumed this success would now enable her to find a job in a New York musical production.

Agnes performing *Ballet Class,* one of her early Degas studies, circa 1931. (Soichi Sunami. Dance Collection, the New York Public Library.)

CHAPTER 10

CONCERT STAGE

MUSICALS OF THE 1920S EMPLOYED WOMEN DANCERS IN LAVISH PRO-
duction numbers. Wearing skimpy costumes to accentuate
their curves, they tap-danced in long lines and raced up and
down glamorous sets, creating fascinating visual effects.

Agnes, hoping to interest Broadway directors in her type
of dance performance, began to audition for agents and
managers in all the theaters. She carried her costumes with
her and performed the same dances she had performed in
her concert. The "bosses," as she called the managers out
front, paid little attention to her, did not understand what
she was attempting to express, and made her feel as though
she did not exist. While she danced, they took care of other
business or sat with their hats on, cigarettes hanging from
their mouths, mumbling that what she did was " 'noncommercial.' "

She tried everywhere, talked to anyone who might be able
to help, but the answer was always the same. "Sorry, we

can't use you" or "You belong on the concert stage."

The de Mille name was no help at all. In some cases it worked against her, because the theater people assumed her famous father or uncle would get her a job.

Agnes was ready to give up. She knew concerts cost a great deal, and there were no guarantees that they would bring in enough money to break even. Mother told her to stop worrying, as she cashed in a few more securities, and decided they would give a concert in Santa Fe. Agnes's close friend Mary Hunter lived there with her aunt, the writer Mary Austin. It seemed the right setting for them to succeed. Mother kept Agnes busy packing her costumes into a trunk and organizing the musical scores, and before Agnes knew it, they were off on the train. Agnes waited eagerly for them to reach the rugged hills and canyons of New Mexico with their vivid, constantly changing colors.

After a grand reunion between Agnes and Mary, Mother put them both to work in the theater she had found. The stage needed cleaning and refinishing, tickets had to be sold, costumes had to be pressed. Agnes rehearsed and tried to ignore the intense summer heat and the fact that Mother had to give away tickets to fill the house. The audience was very enthusiastic as she danced the "character studies" she had presented for her New York concert, and again she received excellent reviews, even if they did not make any money.

Afterward Agnes spent time with Mary Austin. In her books, Mary Austin described what she knew about human behavior and how to keep in close touch with the natural world. That evening she told Agnes to stop feeling sorry for herself because she could not find work, that she should pray and ask God for help, and that she should " 'let the rhythm of the American earth come through what you do,' " just as all peoples have done in their own worlds. For Agnes it was a confirmation of what she was already trying to do in dances such as *'49.*

She went back to New York with new enthusiasm and was able to join another dancer for a December concert. She rehearsed tirelessly, while Mother and a seamstress stitched costumes until the very last moment. Finally it was the night of the concert. Agnes stood waiting in the wings. She wore her familiar yellow tutu and clung to her watering can. The first notes of music were heard. It was her cue to head for center stage, where she became the Degas dancer in *Stagefright.* Later when she danced *Ballet Class,* the audience roared with laughter and Agnes realized the dance she had created was funny and that she was a comedian, although deep down she had thought it a tender ballet illustrating the difficulties a dancer faced. All three concerts were well received, and in high spirits Agnes began to give auditions again. But the managers, who were casting a large revue, still felt she would be better in the concert hall, not performing in their shows.

To hide her unhappiness, Agnes began work on a group of new dances. For *Ouled Naïl,* the dance of a "disappointed stomach dancer," or belly dancer, as we would call her today, Agnes spent time at Greek coffeehouses watching and learning the authentic movements.

Before long she was asked to join Adolph Bolm's troupe of dancers, which was leaving for its annual tour across the country. Bolm had been a fine dancer and choreographer who established a ballet school and touring company. On the road with Bolm's group, Agnes performed three of her own dances, often to empty theaters, and again she felt

Agnes posing for *Ouled Naïl,* the "stomach dancer," 1935. (Harlan Thompson. Beverly Hills Public Library.)

people did not understand what she was doing. In a letter she told Mother, "They sit with faces like puddings all the time I'm on stage. . . . Aside from the fact that I'm a flop everything is jake." The orchestra conductor, Louis Horst, became a great friend and adviser to Agnes as they traveled from city to city by train.

On her return to New York, Agnes saw the Spanish dancer Madame Argentina. Agnes realized there was an important difference between them. Argentina was a magnificent dancer, who used only movement and gesture to transmit her passion to her audience. Agnes saw herself as an actress who danced. She told herself she had to work even harder if she expected to become great.

At the same time, she was given a choreography job and a chance to dance in the show *The Black Crook.* Her new dancing partner, Warren Leonard, had something to say about everything she did. He didn't like the way she danced, dressed, or spoke. He wanted her to stop showing so much feeling and get her steps right. He didn't like having her mother watch their rehearsals. He fought with Agnes about her ideas for dances, with her mother for being too involved in Agnes's life. But more important, Warren was a wonderful dancer who had a great deal to teach Agnes. When she stopped disagreeing with all his complaints and worked as hard as she could, she began to see her own technique improve, and together they appeared for months in the production.

In 1928 a dance critic for the *New York Times* wrote that Agnes had that wonderful quality Charlie Chaplin did: "She leaves you with the same sort of wistful laughter on your lips and the same sort of lump in your throat."

With the praise she was receiving, Agnes felt she was

ready to return to Hollywood to give a concert at the Music Box Theater. She knew it would be a very emotional time, but she wanted the family to see that she was really on her way. Agnes had not seen her father since the divorce, and he had never seen her dance professionally. She arranged for her mother to sit on one side of the theater, her father and his new wife, Clara Beranger, on the other side. When the curtains parted, Agnes danced her heart out. Afterward Clara and William rushed backstage to welcome her into the theatrical world and tell her how much they had enjoyed her dancing. Agnes could not have been happier as she set off for the party Uncle Cecil and his wife, Constance, were giving in her honor.

Her concert received excellent reviews in the newspapers. Uncle Cecil was so excited he offered to back her on a nationwide tour if she could be ready in two months. She knew it had taken her several years to prepare the dances she already had. She could not have a new program ready that quickly. Uncle Cecil withdrew his offer, saying it was now or never.

Her father offered to give her the money for a tour of Europe until a friend cautioned him that European concert managers were known to be dishonest. Fearing that Agnes would be swindled out of the money, her father changed his mind. The success of her concert in Hollywood meant little after being disappointed by both Father and Uncle Cecil. Once again the de Mille name was proving not to be of help to her. Agnes returned to New York, feeling very discouraged, but vowing that she would eventually show them all.

CHAPTER 11

EUROPEAN TOUR

ONE POSITIVE DECISION AGNES MADE ON HER RETURN TO NEW YORK was to find a place of her own to live, no matter how much her mother protested. She was twenty-five and needed to be able to work long into the night without being told to stop and put out the lights. She was more determined than ever to find a place for herself in the dance world as well. She was going to spend the next five years teaching herself to be a choreographer, even if there were no other women choreographers to encourage her or serve as role models.

On her way home one evening in 1931, Agnes stopped to read the latest headlines, only to discover they were announcing the death of Pavlova in Europe. She had been ill with pneumonia and had never recovered. Agnes was crushed. The dancer had been her "vision" ever since she was a child. Now she could no longer hope to receive Pavlova's approval. All she could do was to share her grief with many of New York's dancers at a memorial service and know that all around the world Pavlova was being mourned.

At last, in 1932, Agnes gathered together a group of dancers including Warren Leonard and had them rehearse with her before auditioning for a new Broadway show, *Flying Colors*. Agnes was hired to do the choreography, but she was naive and inexperienced and didn't know how a show was put together. She had never selected dancers before. Casting directors were used to picking young women for their looks. Ballet experience was not considered important. Agnes did not have the confidence to stand up to them and insist on experienced dancers. She ended up with a team of pretty girls who had no classical dance training. They could not understand what Agnes was talking about nor could she create well during rehearsals. She also could not keep people from constantly interrupting those rehearsals. She had no input on the sets being designed for her dancers. The more frustrated she became, the less she was able to accomplish, until she was finally fired. Someone else took over, and the show went on without using most of her work and without giving her credit for the numbers they did use. It was a terrible experience. She had been given an opportunity, and she was not ready for it.

That fall, Arnold Meckel, who managed Madame Argentina, suggested he sponsor concerts for Agnes in Paris because they cost much less than they did in the United States and because he had seen her perform and wanted to give her an opportunity to succeed. After borrowing money from Margaret's new husband, she sailed on the *Ile de France* in October 1932.

Agnes danced in Paris, Brussels, and then London. In London she was introduced to the dancer Marie Rambert. Marie had established the Ballet Club, a school for dancers in an old building in the Notting Hill section, which previously had been a church. It held a practice room with oak floor and barre, a large mirror at one end, and a wood-burning stove at the other. It was always damp and cold, and smelled of wet wool. The building, with its odd stairways and tiny rooms all on different levels, reminded Agnes of the castle she had built when she was a child.

The students performed on a tiny stage, only eighteen feet square. But they were able to perform almost every Sunday evening. There were daily classes, taught by Marie without concern for their feelings; she only cared about their technique. She screamed, she bossed, she lost her temper. " 'Long the arms . . . Down the shoulders . . . Up the head!' " she shrieked.

Marie asked Agnes to stay and perform in the weekly concerts in return for lessons at the Ballet Club. She introduced Agnes to dancers Antony Tudor and Hugh Laing, who would eventually come to the United States to win great fame. In the meantime they were all working as hard as they could for the opportunity to learn from Marie and each other. Agnes still found classes difficult. "Ballet technique is arbitrary . . ." she wrote in her first book. "It never becomes easy; it becomes possible."

Agnes also took private lessons from Antony Tudor, who taught her to "understand the principles behind the technique" and also gave her the opportunity to dance in one of his new ballets because he felt she could "sustain a tragic emotion. [She found the dance] very beautiful and incredibly difficult. There are circular swoonings backward to the floor that nearly knock me out. But I'm honored and gratified to do it. This is my first real recognition as a dancer instead of a mime," she wrote Mother. For very little money Agnes was able to rent an attic room at the English-Speaking Union. In another letter home, she mentioned that it was easier to be poor in England because people tended not to judge you by what you had. She found even the titled and famous dignitaries she met were getting by on very little money.

Her concerts were well received, and she was able to arrange everything without Mother's or a stage manager's assistance—all the business and financial responsibilities, costumes, makeup, lighting, and props.

When Agnes heard that *Nymph Errant,* a musical by Cole Porter, was in production, she boldly offered her services as a choreographer and was hired. The salary was very small, but this time she was given a better opportunity to succeed, and with Gertrude Lawrence as the star, the theater was filled for every performance. Agnes thought Miss Lawrence remarkable in the way she improvised to make each show fresh and unique. The only thing that didn't vary was the way the audience reacted with delight to the Greek and Turkish dances Agnes had created for the great actress.

CHAPTER 12

YEARS IN ENGLAND

FOR ALMOST SIX YEARS AGNES TRAVELED BACK AND FORTH BETWEEN England and the United States. In that time she developed an audience that appreciated her dance tributes to America, her style, and her sense of comedy. She did research at the British Museum, where she read everything she could find about the history of dance and its presence in daily life. She even studied the movements of animals. She wanted her dances to be accurate in every way. During those years she lived sparsely and worked as hard as a whole team of people put together. What she gained was the ability to present concerts on her own, an improved dancing technique, and a tremendous sense of self-confidence. Now she was ready to return to New York.

She wrote to Mother, "I'm starting to do grown-up work and if no one there likes it, I can always come back to where they do." She danced new dances, *Harvest Reel* and Bach's

Gigue. She still complained that she could not do pliés well and that her arabesques were awful. "I'm rump-heavy and too short between knee and ankle." But she knew she could run and walk beautifully. She had "a good foot and a hot bounce" and was a quick jumper. In fact, she could do "sixty-four fouetté pirouettes" on the spot, and she knew that many other dancers could not. But she also knew that being able to whip herself around and around was not enough to make her a great dancer.

In England Agnes made many friends who were dancers, and she also kept in touch with Mother's single-tax friends. She became very devoted to Ramon Reed, a young man who had been paralyzed at the age of seventeen. Agnes called Ramon's disease infantile paralysis in a letter and multiple sclerosis in one of her books. Whatever the medical condition, Ramon was left without the use of his legs, but he loved to have Agnes visit and tell him about her dancing, or what she was reading, or with whom she was having tea that week. He was twenty-two when Agnes met him, a few years younger than she was, and she described him as very handsome with brown, wavy hair and large, dark eyes.

For hours, Agnes and Ramon discussed the classics and their favorite pieces of music. She was able to entice him to leave the house for the first time in years in order to attend one of her concerts. It meant ordering an ambulance to transport him to the theater and being surrounded by curious crowds as he entered and exited. But once in his wheelchair in the theater, he loved watching Agnes dance and he loved the way the audience responded to her.

She also convinced him to get out for an occasional film or picnic. When he told her he had never tasted peanut butter or ripe olives, she rushed to get them for him at the fashionable department store Fortnum and Mason's. He was always thinking of treats to give her because he knew she had very little money to live on. They spent all the holidays together. She rehearsed her latest dances for him, and he read poetry to her. Ramon's home was a haven for Agnes, and she brought to him a taste of the outside world he could not experience. She thought he was a talented writer and hoped to help him publish some of his work. She even developed a dance from one of his ideas.

In the summer of 1935, Ramon was able to travel to the United States, arriving just in time to see Agnes dance at the Hollywood Bowl, where she had been given a generous offer to perform.

The outdoor bowl was quite a contrast to the small stage she was used to at Marie Rambert's Ballet Club. The bowl could seat nineteen thousand people and had a stage over one hundred feet wide. The audience was so far away from the stage they could barely see a gesture unless it was greatly exaggerated. But the acoustics in the bowl were wonderful, and Agnes remembered hearing all the fine musicians who had performed there while she was growing up. In the summers before there were wooden benches, she had wrapped up in a blanket and sat in the sagebrush while the music flowed all around her and the stars overhead bathed her in their glow.

Now that she was actually going to perform on the stage at the bowl, Agnes felt very elated. She rehearsed her troupe of dancers for several days and was very pleased with the way everything came together, despite the heat that built up on the stage every afternoon. They would be dancing *Harvest Reel*, which she had expanded from a solo; *May Festival*, a Czech dance she had created to Smetana's music; and a Gershwin work.

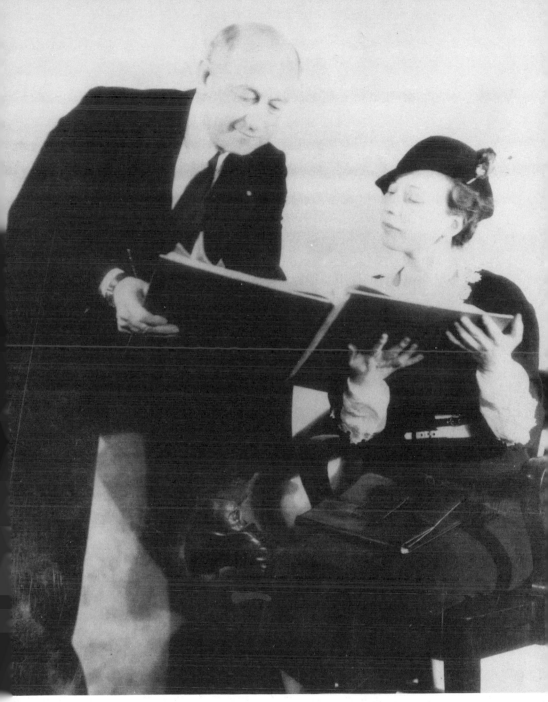

Uncle Cecil and Agnes posing for a newspaper photograph, 1935, when Agnes was in California. (Photographer unknown. Bettmann News-photos.)

The night of the performance, she felt very confident until she began to dance before the large audience. To her dismay, the electrician did not have the proper lighting focused on them and the audience could not see the dancers in *Harvest Reel*. There was no way to reach him and tell him to throw the switch that would turn up the stage lights. When the later pieces in the program were correctly lit, it made little difference because the audience could still not make out the dancers from such a great distance. Agnes felt she had failed miserably. Not only had she lost more of Mother's dwindling savings, but the morning headlines announced, almost gleefully, another de Mille failure.

Fortunately, Ramon was there to help her get through the disappointment and to distract her as she took him to meet everyone at parties in Hollywood and to see the beautiful, scenic landscapes in southern California.

Later that summer, Ramon traveled in a converted automobile to spend time with Agnes in Colorado where she was teaching dance at a summer camp. He went on to visit many sights all over the country, and Agnes felt it had been the happiest time in his life. He returned to England in high spirits, and Agnes joined him there a short time later.

When Ramon became ill in the winter of 1936, Agnes did not want to leave him, but she had a commitment in the United States to choreograph dances for a production of Shakespeare's *Hamlet*. He insisted she leave, and she promised to get back to England to see him as soon as the work was completed. Within weeks, she received a wire telling her Ramon was dead. She kept telling herself she should not have left him. Mixed with her great loss and sadness was her guilt at not being there.

Agnes tried to keep Ramon's memory close to her by

using the copy of *Hamlet* he had given her. During rehearsals of the play, she followed Shakespeare's lines in Ramon's book, always remembering how he had believed in her and encouraged her to work hard because he knew she would someday become famous.

CHAPTER 13

RETURN TO
THE UNITED STATES

IN 1938 AGNES SAID HER FINAL FAREWELL TO ENGLAND AT WATERLOO Station. This time she had no choice. The extension on her work permit was refused that September. War was looming, and the country was sending its visitors home as quickly as possible. As she waved good-bye to friends from the train, her mood was as dark as London's "black November rain." She saw England preparing for war against Hitler's Germany and wrote in her journal, "London became a fortification in two days. Hardly putting down their tea cups with their left hands they picked up guns and gas masks with their right."

Agnes felt sick about what she saw coming in Europe. She also felt she had been fighting her own battles for years, traveling back and forth between the United States and England, trying to find a suitable studio in which to study and create dance, and a responsive audience for which to perform her works. It had always been a struggle, and she was extremely tired. Nearly thirty years old by then, she was

58

sure success had already passed her by. She felt as "stripped as at nineteen except that I had my costumes and my repertoire."

In her despair she was forgetting all that she had recently accomplished. In England she had given her last concert to a full house, followed by the finest reviews she had yet received. She had spent six months working with a group of dancers, three hours every day, preparing an American study that would later become *Rodeo*. The suite was performed in London that April of 1938. Now she could only think about the negatives: Her small group of dancers was separated, her colleagues were beginning new projects without her, Ramon was dead, and she had no money at all.

She wrote to her mother, telling her to find an inexpensive apartment in New York that could double as a studio. Of course Mother wanted Agnes to live with her, but more than ever Agnes insisted she needed her own space in which to live and work. Mother finally agreed and found a studio for her on East Ninth Street, which was perfect even though Agnes knew she could not afford it and would have to depend again on her mother's dwindling savings. Agnes planned to live there very sparsely, with minimal furniture and no rugs, but it had a fireplace where her friends could warm themselves and space for mirrors, a practice barre, and a piano. That was all she needed.

This return was to be a new beginning for Agnes. She vowed to look neater and to be on time, and she made the momentous decision to have her teeth straightened when the dentist agreed to do the work on credit. She began lessons with a group of friends who coached each other, and she was hired by the YMHA to teach two classes a week, for which she would be paid twenty dollars.

After months of searching for work without much luck,

and touring when she could, Agnes received a call from Ballet Theatre, asking her to prepare a ballet for the new company, in two weeks. They even invited her to dance the lead. She immediately began rehearsing *Three Virgins and a Devil,* which she had created and performed in England in 1934, using one of Ramon's ideas.

In the comic ballet, three young women are on their way to worship. Dressed in simple medieval gowns, the Priggish One, the Greedy One, and the Lustful One are fighting among themselves as the curtain rises. They stop bickering to listen to strains of music coming from the Devil, who is disguised as a young musician. No matter how hard they try to ignore it, the Devil's music makes them dance. They can't control their bodies. When they try to keep their hips quiet, their feet won't stop shuffling. If they still their legs, their shoulders and arms gyrate wildly. Suddenly the Devil stops playing his music and tries to entice the women into his cave. Eventually he captures two of them, but Agnes, the Priggish One, keeps escaping until her hilarious struggle to avoid the Devil propels her directly into the mouth of the cave.

After the performance, Martha Graham raced backstage to tell Agnes what a success the ballet had been. " 'In a small, in a tiny, obscure way, this is a classic of its kind, [she insisted] this is a little masterpiece.' " Agnes was particularly encouraged by this compliment because she thought Martha Graham was a genius and one of America's greatest choreographers of modern dance.

In the early years, when Agnes was struggling with her own career, she went to Martha Graham and asked to work with her troupe of dancers. Martha said no. They danced very differently, and she felt Agnes had to find her own way

Agnes with the Devil (Yurek Lazowsky), from *Three Virgins and a Devil,* 1942. (Fred Fehl.)

and not be influenced by the modern dance Martha was developing. Agnes used traditional ballet steps to create a dramatic form, while Martha concentrated on the body's ability to contract and relax, curling itself into a tight spiral and then slowly unwinding. The two women became very good friends, and Agnes valued Martha's impression of her work. If Martha Graham thought *Three Virgins and a Devil* was a valuable ballet, then Agnes knew it was.

Unfortunately, Agnes realized that her wonderful dance was not enough. Audiences were still sparse, money absent, and more importantly, the European war was raging and the United States had entered the battle. Her latest partner had just been drafted into the army.

When that happened Agnes decided concert work was over. She packed up her costumes and tried to find other ways to earn a living. There seemed to be no teaching opportunities. With a form letter, Ballet Theatre returned a new idea she had sent them. Agnes felt they were treating her like a beginner, when actually she had been dancing and choreographing for fourteen years. She had certainly had many opportunities to make it big. They had come to nothing. She had little to show for all the years of struggle. She was continuing to use Mother's money, but now Mother had just suffered a heart attack and Agnes realized she needed to reconsider everything.

It was time for her to find work that would bring in a weekly paycheck. In a few weeks, she decided, she would stop taking classes and stop thinking about new dances. She would get a job at Macy's and pay all her bills and stop taking money from Mother and clothes from Margaret. In just a few more weeks.

Once she had made the decision, she continued to practice and to do her exercises at the barre every single day, just as she had always done. But with her decision to quit, her dancing grew more relaxed and she "bounded and soared" in a way she had never done before. And she kept putting off the day she would apply to Macy's.

CHAPTER 14

RODEO:
AN AMERICAN BALLET

ON HER WAY TO CLASS ONE MORNING, AGNES MET A FRIEND WHO TOLD her that the Russian emigré troupe, the Ballet Russe de Monte Carlo, was interested in performing a new work, perhaps something American. Did she have some ideas for it? Of course she did, she said confidently, even though it wasn't quite the truth. Then she rushed home and locked herself in her apartment. She decided to work on something she knew well—the *Rodeo* studies she had done years before in England. She worked night and day, writing down her ideas, dancing the steps herself, revising, writing some more, all the time drinking one pot of tea after another. After three days Agnes felt exhausted, but she had completed a scenario to present to the head of the Russian ballet troupe, Serge Ivanovitch Denham.

Martha Graham advised Agnes to act as arrogant as possible and not to give in on a single issue. Margaret loaned her

an outfit and a jaunty hat. Mother added her own sugges-
tions for the meeting. Armed with their advice and support,
Agnes was on her way. She kept telling herself she had
nothing to lose. After all, she was quitting after this, anyway.

She entered Denham's office, expecting to meet a bossy,
outspoken Russian. Instead Denham sat behind his desk,
looking elegant and speaking in a quiet, genteel voice. Agnes
described her ideas for doing an American theme, set in
rugged Colorado. He listened thoughtfully while she presented the scenario. He liked it. Yes, they would have a
Western theme, opening the curtains to a bright red barn on
stage. That would be wonderful.

Agnes said there would be no red barn. This was a story
about cowboys and cattle, neither of which are kept in a red
barn, she explained. He still thought a red barn would be
just the thing. Agnes stood her ground. Then she insisted
she would have to be the only choreographer, and that she
wanted the composer Aaron Copland to write the music. She
had heard his work and knew he could write powerful
American themes.

Denham countered that he would require veto power over
her work. Agnes said no again. This went on for a long time
before Denham finally decided to give her a chance, but he
later admitted he had never dealt with a "more opinionated
and disagreeable girl."

Next Agnes met with Aaron Copland to tell him the scenario and see if he would write music for it. He was not
impressed with the story of a cowgirl trying to get her man,
but when Agnes sent him the description of her dance se-
quences, he changed his mind and called to tell her he was
ready to get to work. They sat down together and blocked

out every minute of the ballet. He went back to his studio
to write music that would fit the action. During rehearsals,
whenever Agnes was worried or wanted to change something, he just laughed and kept on with the original version
they had planned.

Agnes was now faced with the challenge of teaching her
steps to Russian dancers who had danced only classical ballet. First she had to retrain them. She wanted the men to
become real cowhands, to walk and ride like cowboys, to use
their strong arms for roping and lassoing. When they entered the stage, she wanted it to seem that they were riding
on real horses, that movement was passing up through their
bodies from galloping animals.

Agnes taught them to make a spasm in their diaphragm
as if they were coughing. That motion would be used
throughout the dancing when they were roping, pulling, and
stretching. She taught them to squint at the burning sun, to
gaze out at the horizon, to act as though they felt hot and
dusty and tired.

Later in an interview, when she talked about *Rodeo,* she
recalled how she had "invented time steps and cowboy
struts . . . added involuntary muscles to them which produced shouts in the body. [She described it as putting] your
whole body into the movement," as ball players and other
athletes do. Tap and ballet were both used in *Rodeo,* Agnes
explained. The two types of dances have no common roots.
"The ballet dancer needs a tight foot and controlled ankle;
the tap dancer, a relaxed foot and loose ankle. The ballet
dancer uses a straight, stiffened knee; the tap dancer a loose
knee." Her dancers had to be able to do everything.

During July, August, and September, Agnes and the Ballet
Russe traveled across the United States, performing dances

Leaping Cowboys (John Kriza, *foreground*) from a production of *Rodeo,* 1960. (Fred Fehl.)

from the regular repertoire. No matter where she was, she followed the war news daily and worried that things were going badly on every front. Yet she continued to perfect the *Rodeo* ballet. Once they were back in New York, it was time to show the ballet to Denham and the other Ballet Russe executives. Mother would also get her first glimpse of the ballet that night. Until then not a soul had been allowed to see any of it. The dancers came dressed in traditional black tights and white shirts, calm and ready to do their best. Agnes was the nervous one. She thought the ballet was good, but what if the others did not like it? She had been very secretive about it during the long weeks of preparation, and now she was afraid they might not understand what she had created.

It told the story of a Cowgirl who dressed like the Cowboys and thought she could ride and lasso as well as they could at their weekly rodeo. The men didn't like her being there and neither did the Rancher's Daughter or her highfalutin eastern friends. Everyone made fun of her.

Agnes was planning to dance the role of the Cowgirl on stage, but for that first viewing she decided to watch with the others and let one of the Russian dancers play her role. She sat in the front of the theater, trying to calm herself, trying not to show her concern. As the ballet began, Agnes felt better. The dancers looked wonderful. Everything was coming together. Even before the piano music ended and the last steps were completed, Agnes could hear cries from the small group in the theater. They had loved it. " 'Thanks God, Agnes,' " one of the Russians called. And then they all began to kiss her. Denham kissed her, Mrs. Denham kissed her, Mother kissed her. They were thrilled, and she was relieved. Now to get everything ready for a large American audience.

For the next few weeks, Agnes continued to practice her role as Cowgirl, while the other dancers took a well-earned vacation. Before she knew it, opening night had arrived. The Metropolitan Opera House was full. People had bought tickets for every seat, and they were not all Mother's friends for a change. Mother had not even spent the day giving tickets away, as she had always done before.

Behind the scenes Agnes waited and worried. The costumes had not yet arrived. She kept telling herself they would come, escorted by seamstresses in taxicabs. But not until the last moment. That was how Karinska always delivered the costumes. At zero hour.

Agnes was not the only one who was concerned. The

dancers also hovered in small groups, whispering and worrying. They were scantily dressed, just waiting to slip into
their costumes. But what if the costumes didn't arrive in
time? What would they do? Should they wear street clothes
or borrow something from wardrobe? With only minutes to
go before the curtain was to rise, Agnes heard the rustle of
tissue paper. The taxicabs had arrived. The costumes were
here! Now, if only they could figure out which pants went
with which shirts and get the right costume on the right
dancer. Somehow they did, and at last they were ready to
dance onto the stage, find their places on the set, and tell
their story.

Copland's music filled the opera house with its plaintive
folk themes, familiar and yet fresh. Beginning with a nostal-
gic mood, the flutes and strings eventually broke into joyous, foot-stamping rhythms, and the audience was caught
up with the action of the ballet.

"If it is possible for a life to change at one given moment,
if it is possible for all movement, growth and accumulated
power to become apparent at one single point, then my hour
struck at 9:40, October 16, 1942. Chewing gum, squinting
under a Texas hat, I turned to face what I had been preparing
for the whole of my life," was the way Agnes eloquently
described that night in her first book.

"This was not a great performance; we gave better later.
Neither was it a great ballet. . . . But it was the first of its
kind, and the moment was quick with birth."

Twenty-two curtain calls followed this performance of
Rodeo. The audience cheered and clapped and whistled. The

Agnes, dancing the role of the Cowgirl in *Rodeo,* 1942. (Maurice Seymour.
Dance Collection, the New York Public Library.)

musicians tapped their bows and stood up, yelling, with the rest of the audience. Stagehands continued to bring out enormous bouquets of flowers for Agnes and the other dancers. There was even an arrangement of freshly picked corn wrapped in red, white, and blue. It was an ovation beyond anything Agnes could have imagined. And it proclaimed loudly that she could continue to dance and to choreograph. With every pageant, every dance, every show, here and abroad, Agnes had been learning to be a masterful choreographer. The success of *Rodeo* had begun many years before, almost from the moment Agnes decided to dance.

Later there was controversy over the similarity between *Rodeo* and Eugene Loring's *Billy the Kid*, first performed in October 1939. Agnes explained that they had been created independently, despite their close timing. Both she and Loring had been trying to use American themes in their work and it was, perhaps, inevitable that they would find similar ways to do so. They had not copied each other's work. Agnes had been in England when she had presented *Rodeo* studies in 1938, but she felt the dances had started even earlier, when she was teaching in Colorado during the summer of 1935. Loring had been working in the United States, trying to use an actual historical figure as the basis for his ballet.

If Billy was a legendary figure, the Cowgirl represented a realistic tomboy, trying to get her man. When critics of the 1980s talk about the role of the Cowgirl, they often find fault with her desperate attempt to attract one of the cowboys. During the morning's rodeo competition, she tries to ride and rope with the men, but is rebuffed by them. That evening, as the dancing begins, the Cowgirl stands off to the side, watching couples dance and spoon. Several times she throws herself to the ground in a wrenching, dramatic gesture to indicate her unhappiness and frustration. She feels left out of everything, much as Agnes always had.

The ballet might have been her own story. Agnes had not been popular with boys. She had always competed with them. She was usually messy and ill kempt and found herself standing outside looking in. She knew the loneliness of not having a special person in her life, and she saw how difficult it was to break into a male-dominated field.

Today's women are entering every field of endeavor. There are female wranglers, fire fighters, and police. Women climb telephone poles, study the depths of the ocean, and fly commercial aircraft. Eventually there should be no areas closed to women. But the need to belong, to be accepted and loved, will be as important in the future as it has always been. That may be the underlying message of the ballet and the reason why *Rodeo* continues to be revived.

CHAPTER 15

INTRODUCTION TO WALTER

THE SUCCESS OF *RODEO* CHANGED AGNES DE MILLE'S PROFESSIONAL life. As one of the first authentic American ballets, *Rodeo* was loved by the public as well as the critics. Its acceptance meant Agnes could continue to dance and to choreograph her own style of dance. It also meant she could forget about Macy's and continue to live the way she always had.

For years she had been in the habit of taking the crowded subway to Carnegie Hall every afternoon for ballet practice. Inside the building she raced up the stairs, to the music of practicing students. Sometimes she heard Leonard Bernstein accompanying a ballet class on the piano or Isaac Stern rehearsing his violin for an evening performance.

Quite out of breath, Agnes would reach the sixth-floor practice room. Suddenly nothing else mattered. She'd stand at the threshold, taking in the broad expanse of space before her. What pleasure it brought. It didn't matter that the floor was splintery and filthy. For her, "Floor space was as irresistible . . . as cool waters to the thirsty." She compared a dancer's emotional reaction to the dance floor with a sculptor's passion for wet clay, or a painter's thrill over fresh paint and clean canvas.

That Wednesday afternoon was no different. As soon as she entered the room she breathed in the atmosphere of sweat and exertion and became a dancer. She took off her street clothes, slipped on her ballet slippers, and rubbed them in the rosin tray before moving with the other students to the barre to begin pliés. For an hour and a half, each of them concentrated on ballet exercises, on stretching arms and legs, on jumping and leaping across the floor. By the time they were finished, Agnes was tired yet exhilarated.

After class Agnes took the subway back to her Ninth Street apartment and had to race to get the door opened before the telephone stopped ringing. It was Martha Graham calling to invite her to a recital that evening and telling her to wear her prettiest dress because she wanted to introduce her to a friend.

Agnes slipped into the slinky black dress she had recently bought on sale. To her own hair she added a hunk of false hair from her costume box. She carefully applied mascara to her eyes and topped her head with a veil so that she would look as sophisticated and dramatic as possible. At Town Hall Agnes saw Martha and Louis Horst coming toward her with a tall, slim, and very handsome man dressed in evening clothes, and soon she was being introduced to Walter Prude.

During the concert Agnes could not concentrate on the performer or the harpsichord music or anything but the man sitting next to her. She kept glancing furtively at Walter, wondering what he was thinking. He seemed to be enjoying the music very much, and she found out later that he did love music and had even given up thoughts of a medical career once he began the study of classical music.

When the concert was over, the four of them went to the Blue Ribbon Hofbrau for sandwiches. Agnes could barely get a word in edgewise. Walter and Martha had too many tales to share, especially since he worked for the concert agency that handled Martha's dance company. But that didn't keep Agnes from interjecting her own comments, anyway, between bites of her juicy club sandwich. She also kept fluttering her eyelids beneath the veil. Walter didn't seem to notice, although he did take her home that evening and made a date to come for tea the next day.

Walter was shocked by his first view of Agnes's studio. Everything was strewn about; there were piles of clothes and papers on every surface. Ballet slippers were on top of books; records were stacked around the room. While he teased her about being a messy housekeeper, Agnes tried to distract him from the chaotic surroundings by telling him everything about herself. She also wanted to know everything about him. He was more diffident, but gradually she pulled out details about his past. He had grown up in Texas, had decided not to become a doctor, wrote stories and poetry. He left her, exhausted by her constant stream of talking. But he returned the next day. Sometimes, Agnes noticed, he seemed far away from her, almost as though he were pulling inward to protect himself. But if she waited patiently, the twinkle usually returned to his eyes.

After they had known each other for two and a half weeks, Walter was drafted into the army and sent to Biloxi, Mississippi. He gave Agnes his journal and all the stories and poems he had written. He was sure he would be killed in the war.

Agnes was more optimistic. She wrote to Walter every day, and in the writing she learned a great deal about herself. Being in love and having someone love her was changing her life. She no longer felt so angry about her situation. She was able to get right to work without dawdling, to treat people more kindly, and to take better care of her apartment and herself.

CHAPTER 16

CREATING A DANCE

"ONCE I'D SET MY TEETH IN THAT, IT WAS LIKE A BULLDOG," AGNES told an interviewer many years later. "You could remove the body from the head, but the jaw was clamped." A determined Agnes continued to study classical ballet and to use it as a foundation for every dance she created. She was not content to stop there, because she had many new things to express. Kosloff, ballet master of the Imperial Russian Ballet, had known she was unique from her very first concerts. "Nothing Agnes does onstage is faintly reminiscent of anything one has seen before in the dance," he said.

From the time she was small, Agnes had danced, but she had also observed the people around her. She watched the way they moved; she studied how they walked across the street, stepped up onto the streetcar, ran to greet a friend. She noticed how they used their bodies to express joy or grief. She was aware of her own motions when she hit long strokes during a tennis match or hiked up the hills. She would bring these movements with their feelings and emotions into her dances.

She would also expand the settings of ballet from castles and kings to country and cowboys, from legends and myths to real life. Instead of stylized dancing where a dancer mimes a gesture of love by placing her hands next to her heart, Agnes had her dancer express love through animated steps and actions in a more realistic and natural way.

In her memoirs Agnes described the way she created a dance. She started by boiling water for a pot of tea; she claimed you don't live all those years in England without learning to drink tea. Then she put a record on the phonograph. Sometimes it was not the music for the dance, because that was not yet created. She let the music flow through her as she drank cup after cup of strong tea. If she had the actual score she played it on the piano for several hours. Then she began to move, blocking out dramatic scenes. She learned about her characters by imagining how they felt, how they moved, even how they walked. She paced up and down, saying she probably covered ten miles every day, in this search for understanding. She called it an "exhausting process, [the] equivalent of writing a novel and winning a tennis match simultaneously."

Once she knew the basic design, she began to compose the actual steps for the dance. For *Rodeo,* she worked directly with composer Aaron Copland, planning the action, and he brought her sections of the score as he finished them.

She gradually learned to visualize large groups of dancers in her head, but she also made drawings and notes, which helped her begin to teach her dancers. She demonstrated the steps, and they imitated her and began to add their own interpretations. Together they worked out the exact steps and gestures, learning from each other, giving and taking, until she was satisfied the story was being told with great clarity. If some of her original ideas didn't work, she threw them out.

Agnes expected the same perfection from her dancers and her students that she expected from herself. "Perish forbid," she would say in exasperation when the class seemed not to understand what she was talking about. She always gave them background information about a dance or an idea. Perhaps she would tell them about the Degas dance she had created and where the ideas came from. When their blank looks told her they didn't know whether Degas was a person or a place, she would grow frantic and swear, "Perish forbid!" It was too much to expect that they might have visited art museums and seen Degas's dancers for themselves. She quickly forgave them if their dancing was superb.

A musical composition is written down using notes on the musical staff and can be passed from performer to performer. Dance notation is quite different. There are three or four systems, each using complex codes to represent motions used by the dancer. It takes several years to learn a system and many early dances were not notated at all. Agnes used her own complex codes to represent steps, the placement of her dancers, and even how they wore their hats. But she also worked with her dancers, telling and showing them what she wanted. Once motion pictures, television, and video cameras became available to record dances, there was no danger they would be lost to future performers.

Agnes toured with the Ballet Russe de Monte Carlo, presenting *Rodeo* in Chicago and San Francisco. At last she reached Los Angeles in the winter of 1942. On the stage of the Philharmonic Auditorium, where once she had seen Pavlova dance those many years before, it was now her turn. There she was, dancing in her own production, with her father in the audience and a full house besides. It must have seemed the most important performance of her life, especially when Pop came to her afterward with "tears in his eyes" and was at last able to tell her of the pride he felt. As a young man he had disobeyed his father's wishes when he chose to become a playwright rather than continue with an engineering career. Perhaps he finally understood why Agnes had disobeyed him. She was as driven by her love of dancing as he had been by his love of theater.

CHAPTER 17

OKLAHOMA!

AGNES HAD INVITED RICHARD RODGERS AND OSCAR HAMMERSTEIN TO see *Rodeo,* because she knew they were beginning a new musical based on the play *Green Grow the Lilacs* and might be looking for a choreographer. The two men were very different. Richard Rodgers was small and compact, with dark black eyes. Oscar Hammerstein, the older of the two, was tall and broad. His lyrics were often called "singable poetry." Rodgers wrote the music first and was willing to try daring, modern ideas. People referred to them almost in one breath as "Rodgers 'n' Hammerstein."

They were very impressed with Agnes's work in *Rodeo* and invited her to meet with them. During her interview, Agnes insisted she be allowed to select her dancers for their ability to dance and act, not because they had beautiful faces or long legs or were friends of the director. She remembered how this had caused her difficulty previously.

They gave her the job, and she began to work "like a pitcher that had been overfilled; the dances simply spilled out of me." In two weeks' time she had designed twice as many dances as would be used. During rehearsals one of the young men came down with German measles, and soon others came down with it. Agnes developed a terrible cough. They danced, sick as they were, in order to be ready for the first tryouts in New Haven, Connecticut, and then traveled with the show to Boston in the spring of 1943. It was a hectic, nerve-racking time. Parts were added, then taken out. Songs were written and rewritten. Agnes continued to rehearse her dancers, but she did not need to make changes in her dances. Still the production was not dynamic enough. At the last moment, Rodgers and Hammerstein wrote a song called *Oklahoma!* with an exclamation point. That was it. They had a new name, and a stronger show was ready to go. They moved cast and crew to New York for an April opening.

Outside the theater on opening night, eager crowds pushed their way through the doorways. Women dressed in glamorous outfits were escorted by servicemen wearing dress uniforms. There were lines at the box office, and taxis stopped at the curb to deliver their occupants. The air was brisk with excitement.

Agnes was unaware of it all. She stood in the back of the theater with Richard Rodgers. "I shall never get over the fear, the stark biting terror of sitting in a first-night and realizing how much depends on chance." She had borrowed a dress from Margaret, but had no time to worry about how she looked. The male lead dancer had injured his foot and insisted on dancing anyway. Several of the women dancers were suffering from exhaustion and leg injuries, too. But the audience could not tell from the performance the dancers gave. "They were roaring. They were howling. People hadn't seen girls and boys dance like this in so long." Here was a story about the West, about its people, its land, its life, and the audience loved it.

Again Martha Graham had much to say after the performance. She reminded Agnes that hers was a "peculiar and unusual gift" and that she had used only a small part of her talent. Martha urged Agnes to be aware of her unique means of expression, because otherwise it would be lost.

There was no question that they were totally different as dancers and choreographers. As a modern dancer, Martha used the bare stage and wrapped herself in plain, flowing fabrics. Agnes loved costumes with ruffles and lace; she wore petticoats under long skirts and fabrics that rustled and moved with her.

Agnes had never been busier or happier. She wrote to her soldier every night, filling page after page with her lovely, small handwriting. After the October opening of *Rodeo,* Agnes had called Walter in Maryland where he was stationed to tell him about the many curtain calls. When *Oklahoma!* opened in 1943, she called him in Omaha to tell him it was a hit. When they were finally able to spend a few days together in Omaha, Agnes showed him every dance from *Oklahoma!* and Walter was quite impressed. He had not really realized what she did, especially from the stick-figure drawings she sent him in most of her letters. They talked about marriage and hoped Walter would get a furlough in the near future so that they could pick a wedding date.

With the tremendous popularity of *Oklahoma!* reporters and journalists demanded interviews with Agnes. Clothing styles, including Agnes's favorite petticoats, were copied from the dance costumes and were seen in shop windows everywhere. Songs from the musical were played on the radio and whistled on the streets. Her mother went to see as many performances as she could, delighted that she no longer was needed to search for a theater, repair the stage, and call all her friends to buy tickets. Often she could not even get a single ticket for herself when she wanted one. It had been her financial and moral support that had kept Agnes dancing all those years. She had continued to believe Agnes could make it even when Agnes had not. From the very first concert she'd pushed and prodded Agnes to keep going, expecting her to succeed. Did she ever think back to her refusal of dance lessons? Probably not, because Agnes was turning out to be more accomplished than either of them could have realized—late start or not.

Rodeo is a ballet that tells its story in two scenes. *Oklahoma!* is quite different. Here is a large musical production in which dances and songs are woven carefully into the plot. Along with several love stories are stories about conflicts between farmers and cowmen. There are humorous, touching moments, and there are frightening, violent scenes.

Jud, the farm workman, is shown to be a disturbed and dangerous man. When he tries to take the young heroine, Laurey, to the dance, stealing her away from her fellow, Curly, there is a battering fight between the two men. A dramatic ballet sequence turns into a vivid nightmare in which all Laurey's fears of Jud are revealed.

Rather than open with a huge dance number as most other shows did, this one begins quietly just as the stage play had, with Laurey's aunt Ella churning butter. Through the ripe cornfields comes Curly, singing about what a beautiful morning it is. Instead of using established stars, Agnes cast

The original dance ensemble performing the dream ballet in *Oklahoma!* (Van Damme Studio, Billy Rose Theatre Collection, the New York Public Library.)

Oklahoma! with dancers who were young and unknown. But not for long.

For months after the opening, everyone wrote about how Agnes de Mille had "conquered Broadway." She had brought dance from the ballet stage to a broader audience and given it equal importance with the words and the music of a theatrical production. A critic said she had become an "Old Master" overnight.

To people who did not know her, it may have seemed as though Agnes became an overnight success. But of course that was not the case. It was 1943, and she had been trying to break into the dance world for sixteen long years. She was thirty-seven years old, a mature, accomplished artist whose work was just becoming recognized in a major way.

Agnes was paid very little, only fifty dollars a week, for her work in the production. With the help of her agent, she signed an excellent contract for the next show she would choreograph, *One Touch of Venus.* Then she was ready to prepare for her wedding.

CHAPTER 18

MARRIAGE

AS SOON AS WALTER HEARD HE WOULD GET A SHORT FURLOUGH IN June, he and Agnes set the date for their wedding and selected Los Angeles as the best location since it was close to his New Mexico base.

Agnes flew to California several days before Walter to begin arrangements. After looking at a number of churches, she selected All Souls Chapel in Beverly Hills for the ceremony. Because they had decided on a small, simple wedding, she told the minister they would not have music. Walter arrived and was adamant that there would be music. He chose an old Swedish wedding march, some Bach and Handel. Together they picked up the ring, a simple gold band, engraved around the edge, and discovered it would not fit. At the last minute they had to find a jeweler who would stretch it.

Finally everything was ready, and at five o'clock on June

14, 1943, they were married. Pop and his wife, Clara, Aunt Constance, and cousin Cecilia served as Agnes's family. Her friend Mary Myer Green was her matron of honor, while Mary's husband, Dennis, was Walter's best man. Agnes wore a brown suit and an extravagantly expensive hat and carried a small bouquet of garden flowers. On Father's arm she almost raced down the aisle to the Swedish march, which she described as "quaint, gay and about as solemn as a field of daisies." Pop had to restrain Agnes and keep her moving at a smooth pace until they reached the front of the church, where Walter was waiting for her. He looked very handsome in his uniform, but Agnes could see how nervous he was, and she decided he probably couldn't even hear the music he had chosen. The ceremony was over very quickly, and then the wedding party met outside on the lawn to offer congratulations.

A few days after the wedding, Agnes wrote her mother, "I've got a good man, Mum, good and dear. I've never been so surely, serenely happy in my life." She tried to describe the ceremony in great detail so that her mother would feel as if she had been right with them. Anna's health would no longer permit her to travel and keep as active a schedule as she always had, and Agnes knew how disappointed she must have felt to miss the wedding; she hoped her letter would help make it up to her.

Over the years Agnes had always written to her mother at length, whenever they were separated, sometimes as many as ten pages in tiny writing on both sides of the ship or hotel stationery. Those letters trained her to be observant of her surroundings and to use her writing skills. She would have them to refer to later when she began to write her books.

Walter and Agnes began married life in Hobbs, New Mexico, a small "oil boom town without sidewalks," eighty miles from anywhere. Agnes tried to ignore the summer sun beating down on them and the hot wind blowing all day and night. She found colorful wildflowers on their high plateau and was able to enjoy the frequent thunderstorms. Besides, New Mexico had good memories for Agnes, and as difficult as it was to work on her dances in the small, stifling room, she did it anyway. Before she knew it, August came. She was forced to leave Walter and return to New York to begin her next project, *One Touch of Venus,* a musical about the goddess becoming mortal.

When she married, Agnes was thirty-seven, several years older than Walter. She had almost decided she would never marry, even though there had been special men in her life. Now she had no questions about her feelings for Walter. She loved him dearly. Still, she worried about how she would divide herself between career and marriage and lamented that it would be so much easier to be "simply a wife or mother, or like great artists, sure and undivided. But all parts of me are set against each other."

When she expressed her concerns to her accompanist, Trude Rittmann, Trude was adamant: " 'Do not question how you are, Agschen. This mixture may be a strength. Use it. You may have something to say for women that the others will not know.' "

Venus rehearsals began in the studio rooms of the American Ballet School. Kurt Weill had composed part of the music before rehearsals began. Mary Martin was the star, but she had never danced classical ballet before. With the coaching Agnes and the other dancers gave her, Mary learned the ballet movements she needed.

Agnes created a special dance for one of the dancers, but when they put the show together, the dance did not fit. Out it went. Again, changes took place all the way through, proving that it is never easy to put a musical together. Some times people are hurt or the pressures become unbearable.

Opening night for *Venus* was no different than any other opening. Agnes did not sit down to watch with the audience. She was always too tense about her dances. Instead she stood at the back of the house, danced every step, conducted every note, and even felt as if she was raising and lowering the curtain. After the Saturday evening opening in Boston, they knew major changes had to be made in the show. The whole staff came together on Sunday morning, and when they left fourteen hours later, they had planned new scenery, new costumes, and new dances. Agnes tried out revision after revision, not feeling pleased with any of them until at last, in the fifth version, she had the dancers move slowly, as goddesses should, and this seemed to do it. They were ready to open in New York, where they got wonderful reviews and audience approval.

Walter was able to get back to New York over the Thanksgiving weekend of 1943. Finally Agnes could take him to see her shows. She bought tickets, and they began the evening with *Oklahoma!* at the St. James Theatre on Eighth Avenue and Forty-fourth Street. For a change Agnes sat with the rest of the audience to watch the production. She was thrilled with what she saw. She felt the cast gave their very best because they knew she had brought Walter to see the show. She kept looking over to note his reactions to a song, to a dance, or to the dream ballet. During the intermission Agnes grabbed his hand, and they ran backstage to congratulate the cast. Walter told her he was amazed. He felt as though he had been watching an opera.

They left the theater and rushed a few blocks away to see the last part of *Venus* at the 46th Street Theatre. This was a completely different experience for Walter. He could not appreciate the show because he had seen very little classical dancing except for Martha Graham's modern dance. Agnes was hurt, but he kept trying to explain that it would take time for him to learn and build a background of dance knowledge just as he had done with music. She would have to be patient with him.

Unfortunately, there was no time. Walter was shipped out two days later, when they had been together for less than ten weeks in all. Martha Graham tried to console Agnes and to remind her how many other women were saying good-bye to their husbands and sweethearts. It was wartime. At least, Martha told Agnes, she could continue to do her work while Walter was away. And she had already shown what good work she could do.

Agnes was alone again. So was her sister, Margaret. Margaret's husband had also been sent overseas, and she moved into Mother's with her young daughter, while Agnes stayed in her studio. The two sisters shared their loneliness with each other and with many other young wives. All of them had stories to tell, a photograph or letter to pass around. Agnes could hardly walk down the street without bursting into tears. Any serviceman she saw reminded her of Walter, and any mother wheeling a baby buggy reminded her of the separation they all faced.

The days passed very slowly as Agnes waited to hear from Walter. She rushed home each evening to collect the mail. It was always the same. Not a word from him. One week. Two weeks. Three weeks went by. The waiting was horrible.

It was almost Christmastime. New York streets were filled with shoppers. Store windows were decorated, carols and bells rang out, but they were wasted on Agnes. She could only think about Walter and worry that she had not heard a word since he left. At last, on Christmas Eve, a telegram arrived. Opening the yellow envelope, Agnes was afraid. Telegrams had become ominous messengers during the war. What would the pasted-on message tell her? With a sigh of relief, she read that Walter had arrived safely. He couldn't tell her where. That was censored information. But at least she knew he was safe.

CHAPTER 19

CHOREOGRAPHER

WORK DID HELP HER THROUGH THE LONG MONTHS OF LONELINESS. Agnes began a new dance for Ballet Theatre called *Tally-Ho.* It was going to be the story of a man who took his wife for granted because he always had his nose in a book. She planned to use the music from a Gluck opera and to set the story in France, with courtly costumes and scenery. She toured with the group and tried to concentrate on composing new dances in between the rehearsals and performances they were giving all around the country. It was not easy, because she never received enough mail from Walter. She listened to war news daily on the radio, saw all the newsreels, and continued to write to him every day. She was not happy with her new ballet. It was not coming together well, and moments before the curtain was to go up on its first showing in Hollywood, she still had not completed the ending. She also had to rely on the help of all her Hollywood friends, who stitched costumes up until curtain time. But it was worth it. Everyone loved the ballet, and best of all, Charlie Chaplin laughed joyously as he watched.

Back in New York, *Tally-Ho* was also wonderfully received. Even though Walter could not be with her, he surprised Agnes by arranging for a box of violets to be sent to her at the theater before the performance, and a blossoming apple tree awaited her when she returned to her studio late that night.

Four nights after her own premiere, she was in the audience for the premiere of *Fancy Free,* choreographed by Jerome Robbins to Leonard Bernstein's music. She called it the finest work she had ever seen in the theater. This was a time of great change in dance, and she and her friends were making it possible.

Agnes analyzed the form her dances took, the way she mainly used diagonal movements and often had a single female figure waiting. She also found she arranged her dancers in circles and used falling motions and sometimes visual jokes. Other choreographers had their own special stamps. And they all influenced each other.

As Agnes and her colleagues worked in their own world of dance, the war was on everyone's mind. There was a great celebration in the United States the day after the Allied troops finally landed in France on D day. On June 7, 1944, no one went to work. Stores closed, churches opened, people reached out to each other and stayed glued to newscasts to hear all the details of the German defeat. The only regret they must have felt was that the invasion had not ended the war.

Agnes was asked to do a show, *Bloomer Girl,* about the Civil War and felt she could use all she had learned about waiting and worrying during wartime. In four days she completed the work and was ready to show it to the "bosses." They hated it. The ballet had no humor, they said. It was sad. The ending was not happy. Agnes knew it was one of the best things she had ever done. She knew the emotions she was expressing were shared by others as well. The bosses continued to say no. Agnes asked for one performance using the dances as they were. Standing in the back of the theater, as usual, she could see how deeply moved the audience was. In every row people sat with bowed heads, especially during the moving Sabbath scene in the second act when the townspeople try to carry on with their normal lives.

One mother unpinned her son's navy wings and presented them to Agnes as she left the theater. The bosses came to her afterward and admitted they had been wrong. The show would be presented as she had created it. Once again Agnes was shown she should trust her own feelings about the way people would respond to her dances.

Walter was still in the service, stationed now in England. Agnes searched for every opportunity to join him there, even though he kept telling her he wanted her to stay safely in the States. In early 1945, Wesley Ruggles, a movie director, came to tell her he was going to London to teach the British how to make a large-scale musical and wanted her to assist him. This would be her chance to join Walter.

While she waited, she arranged shows for servicemen, using numbers from her three shows on Broadway: *Oklahoma!, Bloomer Girl,* and *One Touch of Venus.* Agnes found the reaction of the soldiers very unexpected. Often they yelled out inappropriately during performances. At other times they did not applaud or laugh when they should have. It never occurred to her they might not understand or appreciate dance. She decided their war experiences had made it difficult for them to respond to emotions of joy or beauty. They had seen too much killing during battles. They had lost friends and they had been forced to kill others to protect themselves. Yet Agnes felt it was important for her to keep on giving the performances. It was her way of helping the soldiers leave the war behind them.

She also kept busy refurbishing the studio while she waited to go overseas. She was earning enough money at last to have the rooms painted, the floors refinished, and to buy furniture she found after searching through junk shops. She spent long hours writing to Walter, drawing detailed pictures of everything she purchased and where she placed it. She wanted to share every moment with him and keep home before his eyes.

CHAPTER 20

BACK TO ENGLAND

BY THE SPRING OF 1945, AGNES STILL HAD NOT RECEIVED CONFIRMA-
tion that she would be going to England, so she agreed to
choreograph the dances for Rodgers and Hammerstein's new
show. They were using the play *Liliom* and would call it
Carousel for the musical stage. As with all their musicals, the
team chose stories that dealt with basic truths of life—birth,
love, death—and the pain and joy people share.

Billy, a carnival barker who craves adventure, falls in love
with Julie. They are married only a short time before he is
killed while committing a robbery. He watches from heaven
as his daughter, Louise, grows up an outcast in the community. When Billy is allowed to return to earth for Louise's
graduation, he brings her a dazzling star. Louise is angry at
what her father has done and also feels afraid of him; she
doesn't want to accept his gift. Billy convinces her he is
looking out for her and wants her to have hope and faith in

her life. The music is lovely and sentimental, the story sad and touching.

After opening in New Haven in March 1945, there was more hard work, with changes being made in the score and in the dances. The cast traveled next to Boston, where Agnes watched the spring bulbs appear and the trees leaf out. She wondered if it was spring for Walter. This was the second year they had been separated, and she was horrified to realize she could no longer remember what his voice sounded like.

Concern for Walter's safety was always on her mind even when she tirelessly worked on the show. At any moment she kept expecting to hear that she could leave for England to be with him. She knew how much he would enjoy *Carousel* and wished he could have been with her for the New York opening when Bambi Linn, who played the daughter, received such hearty ovations that the show had to stop. That was a rare event in a musical.

On May 8, 1945, the German army was defeated, but the war with Japan was still being fought in the Pacific. When Agnes finally received permission to go to England, she purchased an airplane ticket and left on June 14, her second wedding anniversary, eager for her reunion with Walter.

Arriving in London, Agnes was stunned to see what war had done to her beautiful city. Homes were demolished. Parks were empty of flowers, the lawns had turned brown, and iron fences had been removed for scrap metal. Wearing her fashionable hats, Agnes stood out wherever she walked because English women had not been able to worry about their wardrobes during the long years of bombings. Food and shelter had been their only concerns.

Once she was settled in a flat, she set to work on the

dances, but found it difficult to get inspired by the music and lyrics of Ruggles's musical. She had signed a contract without seeing anything because she had been so eager to get to Walter. Now she could not reach him by cable, by telephone, or by letter. Weeks passed without any word from him.

At last, in July, Agnes finally received a letter from Walter telling her that he didn't know when he would be able to join her, that it might be better if she broke her contract and went home to wait. She was heartbroken. That day she cried until she was exhausted. Finally, she realized she had dances to create no matter how upset she was. She put a Schubert recording on the phonograph and tried to concentrate. When the doorbell rang, Agnes opened the door, her eyes and nose still bright red from hours of crying. In front of her stood a soldier, handing her the evening newspaper. That soldier was Walter.

It had been almost two years since Walter and Agnes had seen each other. Now they would have only twelve days together before Walter had to ship out for the Pacific, where the war was still being fought against Japan. But they were twelve wonderful days in which they shared their feelings and news of all that had happened to their family and their friends.

That August, atomic bombs were dropped on Japan, and the war came to an abrupt end. Walter was shipped back to the United States, while Agnes still had four months left on her English contract.

In New York, Walter looked for a job during the day and went to see all of Agnes's shows at night. In London, Agnes walked the city streets, her mind filled with memories from earlier years, despite the many bombed-out buildings and piles of rubble all around her. She also tried to imagine what life had been like for Walter when he had been there. She missed him terribly, but knowing she was pregnant with her first child was helping her get through the remaining weeks.

Agnes kept wondering what the future would bring and how she could continue to work once the baby was born. She dreamed of taking the baby with her to rehearsal sessions at Carnegie Hall, where she would leave it, hanging on the wall papoose-style, while she worked at the barre. She thought of all the other things she would do. She decided to begin work on a new ballet. She planned to start writing her memoirs. She would even learn to cook. Then Rodgers and Hammerstein wrote, asking her to choreograph and direct their next musical, *Allegro.* She did not need to worry about the future. She would be able to do it all.

She counted the days until it was time to board a small freighter and head home in November 1945. That winter brought terrible storms on the ocean, with torrential downpours and huge waves. Everyone was seasick, except Agnes. She was sure it had to do with her genes from her grandfather Henry George, who had twice sailed around the world, and from the fact that she was carrying a child who would also love the sea. After sailing for seventeen days, they finally reached Pier 57 in Manhattan. From the railing Agnes could see Mother taking one hand out of her fur muff to wave, and Walter, still dressed in uniform, running toward the ship. They were together at last, and for them the war was really over.

CHAPTER 21

BABY AND BOOKS

AGNES GAVE BIRTH TO THEIR SON, JONATHAN, IN THE SPRING OF 1946. What should have been a joyous occasion for Agnes and Walter turned into a sad, worrisome period. For the first five years of his life, the baby was quite ill with a congenital condition requiring repeated surgery and causing many recurrent infections. From moment to moment they were never sure if Jonathan would survive.

At the same time, her mother's health was growing worse, and Agnes brought her to the studio to live with them. Anna died a year after the baby's birth. She had lived long enough to get to know her young grandson and to learn of Agnes's success with a new musical, *Brigadoon.* She had also received the good news that her biography of her father would be published.

Her mother's death was a terrible loss for Agnes. As she had always done, she decided to use the feelings of grief in her work. She began to write her memoirs and she began a ballet filled with ominous moods of despair over the loss of her mother and her anxiety about Jonathan. She also included the frustration she had felt for those many years when success had eluded her.

For the 1948 ballet, called *Fall River Legend,* Agnes told the story of Lizzie Borden, who, in 1892, was reputed to have hacked her parents to death. Although Lizzie was found not guilty by a jury in Fall River, Massachusetts, the newspapers of the day sensationalized the crime and the trial. Young children repeated the anonymous rhyme:

> *Lizzie Borden took an ax*
> *And gave her mother forty whacks;*
> *When she saw what she had done,*
> *She gave her father forty-one.*

Agnes decided to tell the story of a young woman who could find no way out of her terrible life except to kill her harsh father and stepmother. She saw Lizzie Borden's existence as one of desperation whether she had been guilty or not. To get her dancers into a somber mood she told them, "Pretend you're ugly, that you have a thick neck."

There was a great deal of controversy over her use of such a subject and the fact that she changed the outcome of the case, but nothing could take away from the powerful reactions the dance created in its audiences. The ballet opened with an all-male jury accusing the young woman of murder as she stood under the gallows. The stage set was a stark, wooden construction that began as the gallows and gradually changed into the family's house. Three chairs sat in the parlor: a straight chair for Lizzie, rocking chairs for her fa-

A scene from the ballet *Fall River Legend*. The gallows *(left, rear)* appears to be part of the house; the chairs are the only visible furniture. (Louis Melancon. Library of Congress.)

ther and stepmother. Lizzie did not need a rocker. Her agitation kept her body moving. The family sat rocking back and forth, back and forth, to the point of monotonous madness, and the scene was set for the horrors to come. During the killings the sky turned bloodred, and ominous music added to the horror.

Agnes's first book, *Dance to the Piper,* had none of the heavy sadness found in the *Fall River Legend.* She wrote with wit and verve, using words in the same magical way she created dances. You can almost hear her rich voice describing how close her family had been, how much love there was as she grew up, and how those bonds were the "music of my childhood." This first memoir began on scraps of paper, napkins, any handy piece of paper on which she could jot ideas. She felt she had a story to tell about her family and her early struggles to become a dancer. She had learned the "rhythm of language" from an early age because her family spoke well and surrounded themselves with others who also respected the written and spoken word.

She insisted she wrote most of her book in the corner drugstore or while sitting in the hospital waiting room. She switched from using napkins and laundry lists to ledgers and notebooks. She found the hours between four and six A.M. the best for doing revisions. She also created much of her choreography then. Her long, detailed letters had taught her to observe the outside world. Her diaries had been a place for her feelings. Now her books joined her observations and her emotions to become important records of the times and her place in them.

Jonathan was becoming a healthy, hearty young boy, and Agnes was combining marriage, motherhood, and career quite nicely. The family spent as much time as possible at Merriewold, taking care of the house and the garden and enjoying the relaxed country atmosphere; life in New York was hectic and pressured for all of them.

In the 1950s Agnes added television to her list of accomplishments when she appeared in the Omnibus television presentations. Agnes spoke about the history of dance and then introduced dances from countries around the world: the Congo, Scotland, Siam, Spain. Remember how an enthusiastic eleven-year-old Agnes had presented dance pageants from around the world in her backyard? The only difference

Agnes, Walter, and their son, Jonathan, circa 1960. (Photographer unknown. Dorathi Bock Pierre Dance Collection, Beverly Hills Public Library.)

now was that during the intervening years she had studied everything she could about the subject.

Now that her work was well known, Agnes received more requests for her choreography than she could meet. She did choose to create dances for a number of musicals, such as *Paint Your Wagon, Gentlemen Prefer Blondes,* and *Goldilocks.* Many of these shows were made into moving pictures that reached even wider audiences, although some people felt there was never the same excitement on screen as there was in the live stage production. At the same time, she was creating strong, new ballets: *The Four Marys, A Rose for Miss Emily,* and *Texas Fourth.*

Agnes no longer had to worry that her audiences did not understand the meaning of her dances. She had touched a universal core of feeling in her ballets, as well as her musicals, and even Uncle Cecil finally admitted that she had made the "name of Agnes de Mille world famous as [that of] the foremost American choreographer of our time."

When Agnes was almost sixty, she used her great knowledge about dance to write a book for young dancers in which she stressed the importance of the dancer's body. "You cannot buy your instrument, like a violinist or pianist. You must make it, and you must make it during the time your body is growing."

She questioned whether a dancer could have a dancing career and also attend university as she had. She thought not. Schools that combined academic education with dance training were very rare when she was growing up. They are still the exception. Yet she is a perfect example of a highly educated woman using that education to great advantage in her art and in every other phase of her life. She continued to write books about dance and about the story of her life in one volume after another.

She and Walter also valued an education for Jonathan, who received advanced degrees in American history and then went on to teach at Emory and Harvard universities.

In 1966 Agnes was invited to take a dance group to the Soviet Union. The Russian audiences responded to *Fall River Legend* more positively than to *Rodeo* or any of the other dances performed. Among the Russian dancers she met at that time was Mikhail Baryshnikov, who later defected to the United States, where he has become an important figure in the American dance scene. He danced the role of the Devil in Agnes's *Three Virgins and a Devil,* and he remembered how impressed he had been with her work when he had seen it performed in Russia.

STROKE

AGNES LONG HAD DREAMED OF ESTABLISHING A SCHOOL IN WHICH students would study dance as well as academic subjects without having to give up one for the other. At last, in the 1970s, she founded the Heritage Dance Theater at North Carolina School of the Arts. To build financial support for the program, she planned to give a New York dance concert in the late spring of 1975. She selected the dancers and wrote an elaborate script to describe their motions and meanings.

After weeks of rehearsal, May 15, 1975, finally arrived. That morning Agnes went to the Hunter College Playhouse laden with her notes, her new red gown, and its matching shoes and jewelry. She was tired and worried about getting all the details worked out, but she knew it was always that way on the day of a performance. She rehearsed with the dancers most of the day and, shortly before the opening-night curtain was to rise, sat down in the front row of the theater to take care of some last-minute paperwork. Once that was done she planned to go backstage and get dressed for the gala event.

As she held a pen in her hand, ready to sign a dancer's contract, Agnes suddenly found her right hand would not work. Then she realized she could not feel her right leg. She knew something was terribly wrong. She rarely paid any attention to her health. The doctor had given her pills to take for high blood pressure. Sometimes she took the pills, sometimes she forgot. Now her neglect was catching up with her.

Someone ran to call for her doctor, whose hospital was very close by. Within minutes he arrived at the theater. After checking her condition, he helped carry Agnes into a waiting ambulance. He told her there would be no program that night. Almost relieved, she closed her eyes and let the experts take over. At the hospital they did a brain scan with a brand-new piece of equipment called a CAT scanner. It showed a hemorrhage seeping into her brain. Blood in her spinal fluid also confirmed the diagnosis.

The doctors told Walter they did not expect her to live through the night. He called Jonathan, who was teaching in Cambridge, and her sister, Margaret, in Easton, Maryland, and told them to hurry to New York. Agnes was dying. When they entered Agnes's hospital room the next morning, expecting the worst, there she was, sitting up in bed, enjoying her breakfast. Unfortunately, her condition did not stay that positive. The bleeding in her brain continued, and the medical staff and her family hovered over her with great concern.

At last the hemorrhage stopped. But Agnes had suffered a severe stroke. She was unable to use her right hand and her right arm. Even her eyes did not work. She could not find the proper words to express herself. She grew furious when Walter or the nurses did not understand what she wanted.

After the first few weeks, her fury turned to frustration. There were times when she wanted to give up. Her right arm was useless. Her right leg had no feeling. She had been right-handed before the stroke. Now it took every ounce of energy she had to do one tiny thing, like sit up or put on her glasses with her left hand. She railed against her useless limbs. Sometimes she felt as if she could not face the future as she was.

But she also knew she was not ready to give up. She wanted to live, and she was going to fight to make her body work again. She called upon the determination she had used in dancing. She would not let herself feel discouraged for even a second. "I will" became her watchword, not "I can't."

After a month in the hospital, struggling with physical therapy, hand therapy, medicines to reduce bleeding, medicines to prevent future clots, her eyes began to work again. She could even see the dreadful picture on the opposite wall of her room, but she was not yet able to read. When at last she could read, she asked her friend Mary Green to bring the pile of papers she had been collecting for her latest book. It was to tell about her early years at Merriewold, and because they had been such happy years, she thought it would make her feel good to work on the book. It turned out to be slow and frustrating. Her left-handed writing was still almost illegible. But even worse, she could not hold on to the pieces of paper. They tended to slip off the bed or to get lost in the blankets, and then she would have to ring for help. The nurses would find and sort her notes and arrange them in a neat pile on her bedside table where she could see the stack growing. She called it a "small compost heap of loose papers [which became a] promise" for the future and kept her going.

Sometimes there were evenings so special Agnes was almost able to forget she was in the hospital. The golden glow of sunset would transform her room into an old English painting, and she and her nurse would fall under its temporary spell. For their thirty-second anniversary, Walter gave her a party in a hospital dining room. Surrounded by dear friends, they celebrated their long marriage and also the fact that Agnes would live.

The therapy sessions never stopped. Part of her work was done at a wooden barre. But now she did not have the use of her body. Her paralyzed right side prevented her from moving along the barre easily. It dragged her down. It could not keep up with her wishes. She dreaded the hourly session because she was afraid of falling, and often she did tumble on her face. Before the stroke, she had moved almost unconsciously. Her brain had sent messages to her hands and arms, and they had functioned superbly. Now her brain was damaged and could not get the messages through. When one of the physicians asked her to rise on her toes, she could rise on her left toe. The right foot would not move. He told her she would never be able to do better than that. "His remark stung me. In two months I was doing four relevés and in six months I was doing eight." His words had been a challenge to her.

She still retained the sense of discipline she had known since childhood, combined with the physical discipline she had learned from dancing. Mother had expected her to sit and do her needlework and sewing with care and skill. As she and Margaret went on in school, they were expected to achieve the highest grades and become the best at whatever they did, whether it was in sports or in music or in a job.

If it had taken two years to learn to walk the first time, she knew it might take her two years to learn to walk once again. After all, it had taken her twelve years of dancing before she could get on point and do fouetté pirouettes. It had taken twelve or fourteen years of practicing two hours a day before she became a proficient pianist. She knew how long it took to accomplish important skills.

She kept making bargains with herself. "If I had the use of my thumbs I'd give up my foot. If I had part of my right hand . . . [Or another time,] If I could have my hand for an hour a day! . . . [But then she would chide herself,] "Stop it!" and did.

She worried constantly about her garden at Merriewold because there was no one to tend it. She was certain it would turn to weeds overnight. When friends sent her huge bouquets of peonies, tiger lilies, or moss roses, the flower arrangements made her miss her own flowers even more. If only she could get to Merriewold, she knew she would feel better.

Agnes had several setbacks caused by additional blood clots in the leg and neck. Fortunately she was able to tolerate drug therapy and surgery, but after three and a half months of hospitalization, her spirits were beginning to flag again. Her doctor decided to send her home because he feared that Agnes would not get well in the hospital, that she needed to be in a more positive environment, surrounded by her family and familiar objects. Home would be the best medicine of all. Walter, who had been a terrible pessimist in the past, now became her greatest supporter. He assured Agnes that her illness had been " 'the making' " of him. When she first came home, Walter was always there, urging her on and finding something to make her laugh.

She worked with several different physical therapists in the hospital, and one of the therapists continued to give her treatments at home, where they put in a ballet barre to allow her to practice walking slowly, forward and back.

She learned she could do only one thing at a time. Her greatest achievement became the trip across the bedroom and into the bathroom on her own. This, after she had been able "easily to do one hundred forty-four relevés, sixty-four fouetté pirouettes, and hold prolonged balances on full point."

When she was finally able to take the trip to Merriewold, she tried not to feel discouraged by the neglected state of her gardens. Instead she sat in the sun and thought of the past. She remembered what it had been like to be ill there as a child, when Mother tucked a quilt around her on the living-room sofa. Often she had looked at Mother's precious Kate Greenaway books, but most of the time Agnes had lain there and listened to every sound in the forest and every move-ment in the kitchen. It was that kind of concentration she needed to regain. She had to call on that tremendous ability to be still and to wait, a quality she had known since child-hood. Now she needed to learn to be content in the single moment and the single act.

In *Reprieve,* the book she wrote about her illness several years later, she described that feeling as similar to what Buddha referred to when he said, "I am awake." In a sense, Agnes felt she had died during her hospital stay and was now beginning anew, just like a small child.

CHAPTER 23

NEW CHALLENGES

IN LOOKING BACK, AGNES REALIZED WHAT A TREMENDOUS INSPIRATION her son, Jonathan, had been during her illness. After his own early years of sickness, he had grown up to be a sensitive, caring young man. He and Walter had found a new closeness with each other as they worked to help Agnes regain her physical strength.

When Jonathan was married on Thanksgiving Day in 1975, Agnes was able to dress up in an elegant long robe Martha Graham loaned her. She wasn't prepared for the sadness she would feel when she could not dance with her son after the ceremony, but had to watch him waltz with his new mother-in-law. "I wanted to dance him proud. I had to yield my place. Right then I grew old."

As discouraged as Agnes felt at times, she continued her therapy sessions at the hospital several times a week, with the same diligence with which she had attended her ballet classes at Carnegie Hall. Slowly she walked back and forth

112

at the barre, did exercises on the floor mat, some on all fours. One momentous day she realized she could sense the weight of her right foot on the ground. She was startled and thrilled.

Then her doctor suggested a brace for her right leg, and she was horrified. How could she have come to this after all the years she had been so mobile? When it turned out the brace gave her much more stability and allowed her to walk more easily, she decided she could put up with it. Especially if she could conceal it under colorful silk pants with long, matching tunics. A dressmaker made her several outfits, and Capezio made matching slippers to cover her poor, twisted foot.

That fall she raged when she lost the opportunity to do two new Broadway shows. After all, there was a time in the forties when she had been the number one box-office attraction for three years running. At that time directors had come to her first when they needed a choreographer, and she could choose the shows she wanted to do. Still she lamented that her career had not been as successful as she would have liked it to be, that she had not created enough serious dances. With the stroke she began to forgive herself and to realize that she could not change the past, nor did she want to return to the theater, with its intense pressure. She had to find a new way to use her talents. She may have been left with half a body, but her mind was still whole.

Her first chance came when American Ballet Theatre approached her with plans to present some of her work at Lincoln Center. She felt revitalized by coaching the dancers and was very moved during the performance when the mayor of New York presented her with the Handel Medallion in honor of her contribution to the artistic community.

She also continued working on her manuscript, which was

to become *Where the Wings Grow* in 1978. She spent time
every day revising, writing new sections in left-handed
longhand, or speaking onto a tape that was later transcribed
by her friend Mary Green. It did make her feel good to relive
the early years at Merriewold, to think about all the fascinating people she had known there, and to recreate the
beauty of the setting. It was a healing process for her emotions as well as her body.

She was asked to attend many galas all over the United
States and Canada, and in October 1976, when Martha Gra-
ham was presented the Medal of Freedom in Washington,
D.C., Agnes was invited as a special guest.

During the night Agnes became ill again. She was rushed
back to her doctor in New York, who hospitalized her for a
heart attack. As soon as she began to feel better, she insisted
the doctor let her leave the hospital; she was needed at *Rodeo*
rehearsals. The doctor would not release her in time for the
performance being given by the Joffrey Ballet, but Walter
reported it was a huge success. She heard the news with
mixed feelings. A huge success, but without her. It didn't
make her feel very needed.

She was out of the hospital in less than three weeks and
eager to begin a new project with the Joffrey. The company
planned to help her present *Conversations About the Dance,* the
program that had been interrupted by her stroke. She asked
her neurologist, Dr. Plum, if he thought she was up to giving
the performance. " 'You cannot live your life as though you
were going to die,' " he told her. " 'You will die, of course,
and possibly sooner now than before. But you must live as
though you will live.' " That's all Agnes needed to hear. She
would finally give the program she had started to give two
and a half years before.

It was up to her to show the dancers what she wanted, and her body would no longer allow this. She had to find the words to explain where the foot should be placed, how high the jump, how long the pause. She chose assistants who could interpret her ideas and almost read her mind. While it was taxing for her, she had always been precise, and she found the dancers quick to understand. They had all been trained in classical ballet, but it didn't take them long to pick up folk dance steps and the other movements Agnes expected. Suddenly it was time to stop rehearsing. The big night had come.

Agnes had to feel nervous. No matter how hard she tried not to think about what had happened before, it was always in her thoughts. This time they were appearing at the City Center Opera House, which had almost three thousand seats, compared to Hunter College's seven hundred. In the dressing room, she very slowly put on the same red dress she had planned to wear originally—for good luck. She smoothed her hair back, did her face carefully, and then took her seat on the stage. Just before the curtain opened, she took a deep breath, and from the minute the audience heard her speak they were with her, laughing and responding to her words. She could feel their support throughout the evening, and when she gave the last calls for the *Rodeo* square dance, she held out both hands as naturally as she had always done, almost forgetting that her right arm had not moved since her stroke. Then she rose for the curtain call to stand without her cane or the supporting arm of a friend, almost as though her adoring public was offering her their protection. She stood, raising both arms in gratitude to them.

After that she traveled to California, where she presented the same program at the Greek Theater in Los Angeles and the Opera House in San Francisco. During the evening Agnes emphasized the immigrant influence on American dance. She explained that "Jacobean dances and the Minuet were samples of ballroom dances, brought to the States from England and France. In America's frontier these evolved into the Square Dance." She told how the original Irish jig became the tap dance when blacks added African elements of "torso movement and a syncopated upbeat." Most important, Agnes described the way the human body allowed dance movements to develop and said that we are the only species to dance "as an expression of emotion."

The following year she created a new ballet for the Joffrey, *A Bridegroom Called Death,* with music by Franz Schubert. It begins with a young woman's joyful dancing until a sudden storm approaches. The mood darkens along with the sky, and the dancing changes from a casual folk style to an extremely dramatic ballet. Many interpreted it to be her own story of being struck down by illness at a very productive time in her life.

Agnes didn't stop at creation. Her parents had early taught her to share their "passion for social justice" and concern for causes. Beginning in the 1930s, as president of the Concert Dancers' League, she worked to develop legislation that would allow concerts to be presented on Sundays and to improve wages and other working conditions for dancers. As recently as in June 1979, Agnes appeared before a Senate subcommittee to request money for the arts. She called art a wonderful therapy and one of the best ways for people to communicate. She felt her own recovery from the stroke was a perfect example.

Using statistics, Agnes showed the senators that our country allowed only $1.10 for art endowment for each citizen, whereas England paid $4.00, France $10.00, and Denmark $20.00. She understood it was a difficult time to ask for money, but told them to think back to the dark days of the London bombings during World War II. The great pianist Myra Hess played music for any people who came to the National Gallery to listen. After the war, when money was even scarcer in England, the Sadler's Wells Ballet produced *Sleeping Beauty* and brought it to America in 1946. Agnes told them that people need art even more when their world is being assaulted.

In October 1979, Agnes was presented with the Arnold Gingrich Memorial Award for outstanding individual achievement in the theater, and the following year, President Carter chose her to be the recipient of Kennedy Center Honors. Looking elegant, her silver hair swept back from her face, garnets at her neck, she sat in the balcony next to the opera star Leontyne Price, listening to her colleagues' praise and watching young dancers from her Heritage Dance Theater perform in one of her joyful ballets, *Texas Fourth.* With both hands she threw the dancers kisses as the audience gave them a rousing ovation. It was a glorious moment for Agnes de Mille to reap the rewards of her career and to know that her work would be carried on.

The following spring, as part of the Kennedy Center award, Agnes was interviewed for two and a half hours by talk-show host and actor Dick Cavett. She spoke brilliantly, recalling every detail of her career. She even quoted long lines from dramatist George Bernard Shaw, whom she had met in London.

Dressed in gold silk pants with a matching tunic, her makeup perfect, she moved her left arm with the grace of a dancer as she described the people and events in her past. At one point she raised her left leg high, arched her foot, and pointed her toes to perfection. You could almost hear her saying, See, I haven't lost my technique even though my right leg refuses to work.

In July 1986, she received another major award—the Medal of Arts from President Reagan—along with singer Marian Anderson, writer Eudora Welty, and her friend, composer Aaron Copland. It was only the second year the awards had been presented, but the president explained that the tradition of awarding excellence in the arts went as far back as President John Adams, who insisted he "studied war so that his sons might study commerce and agriculture, so that their children could study painting and poetry."

CHAPTER 24

THE INFORMER

AGNES CONTINUED TO WRITE BOOKS AND TO PRESENT REVIVALS OF HER
early ballets. Mikhail Baryshnikov, the Russian dancer who
had become artistic director of American Ballet Theatre,
came to Agnes with a proposal to revive *Rodeo.* He had first
seen Agnes's work when he was a young student in Russia,
and he continued to be her admirer after he defected to the
United States. Agnes thought very highly of his dancing and
the way he was guiding the ballet company. She suggested
he let her prepare a new ballet for ABT's fiftieth anniversary
celebration in May. She convinced him that she needed the
challenge of creating something new rather than continuing
to repeat the past.

Many years before, Agnes had choreographed Irish
dances for the Broadway show *Juno and the Paycock,* and now
she wanted to explore new ideas. She wanted to create a
ballet that would deal with the emotional problems people

face in a country long divided by war. She insisted it would not be a political ballet. She would not take sides. Her concern was for the people on both sides whose lives were filled with poverty and terror and death.

Every morning she went to a rehearsal room at the Joffrey Ballet School, which was quite near her apartment. There she developed her ideas for the ballet with a group of dancers she had hired. After two years of preparation, she moved to ABT, where she taught the individual dances from her wheelchair with the aid of an assistant. She was as exacting about what she expected from the dancers as she had always been. She encouraged them but always expected more—a higher lift, a stronger emotion, a faster leap—just as she continued to expect the impossible from herself. Baryshnikov told a reporter, "She accomplished more from that wheelchair than most other choreographers do running around all over the stage."

That May evening in 1988, when the curtain fell on *The Informer,* the audience rose to honor Agnes with their applause and their appreciation for a lifetime of accomplishments. Almost fifty years earlier her first ballet, *Rodeo,* had received twenty-two rousing curtain calls on the stage of the Metropolitan Opera House in New York City.

There are three main characters and a large corps de ballet in *The Informer.* Tension begins the moment the Young Fighter tears down a wanted poster of himself. It continues to build through the frenzy of Irish step-dancing, in which legs and feet are in constant motion while the arms and upper body remain still. The powerful movements and stirring music maintain a chilling sense of fear throughout until the ballet ends with betrayal and death by hanging.

As an idealist, the Young Fighter wants to defend his

The Girl (Kathleen Moore) and the Wounded Veteran (Victor Barbee) in a joyful moment from *The Informer*. (Steve Ringman. *San Francisco Chronicle*.)

country while trying not to get caught by the enemy, the British police force called the Black and Tans. Agnes understood the role of a fighter. She had confronted enemies all along the path of her career, at first in her own family. Then there were the stage managers and theater bosses, the social conventions and critics, and the latest attack from within her own body.

The Wounded Veteran is forced to dance and lift his partner with his one whole arm, leaving his leather-covered stump hanging uselessly. Agnes understood his plight. She had learned to exist with only one arm. She also understood the horrors of war. She had seen what the bombings had done to London, and she knew about the death and destruction others faced whenever there was battle.

In the ballet, both young men fall in love with the Girl, her striking red hair flowing as she dances with each of them. She seems to be more in love with her country than she is with either of them. This is a self-assured, confident young woman who has to make difficult choices. She is no longer the shy, fearful Cowgirl who had danced in, and created, *Rodeo.*

Like her characters, Agnes had faced life and found it full of conflict. She set this ballet in a time of hardship and warfare, where the enemies were unseen and the wails of the people were soundless. She used the repetitive beat of Irish dancing to serve as a vivid reminder of the country's suffering.

Perhaps Agnes de Mille was not dancing on her feet any longer, but her creativity had not been stilled by the stroke that limited her movement. She still thought of herself as a dancer and always would. That is what she had been from the beginning, and that is what she wanted her tombstone to read: DANCER.

NOTES

Chapter 1

Throughout the book you will find the word *theater* spelled with the *er* ending, but sometimes it will be written *theatre*. The British often use the latter spelling, and many groups have chosen that usage for the names of their dance troupes.

In fact . . . moment. "One Day in Pictures Was Enough for Agnes de Mille," *Boston Globe,* 30 March 1930.
"straight into the . . . toes." Angelica Gibbs, "Profile—Choreographer," *New Yorker,* 14 September 1946.
"Stark naked," *Agnes, the Indomitable de Mille,* "Great Performances" on PBS, January 1980.
"You'll catch cold!" Ibid.
"slowly wheeled around . . . wine." Ibid.

Chapter 2

"modest" and "lady" Agnes de Mille, *Where the Wings Grow* (New York: Doubleday and Co., 1978), 60.

"dashing . . . lean," Ibid., 55.

"referred to . . . good-night.' " Agnes de Mille, *Speak to Me, Dance with Me* (Boston: Little, Brown and Co., Atlantic Monthly Press Books, 1973), 7.

"teas or receptions" Agnes de Mille, *Dance to the Piper* (Boston: Little, Brown and Co., Atlantic Monthly Press Books, 1951), 10.

"The foot . . . foot." Agnes de Mille, *America Dances* (New York: Macmillan Publishing Co., Inc., Helene Obolensky Enterprises, Inc., Books, 1980), 2.

Chapter 3

"danced off . . . earth," *Agnes, the Indomitable de Mille.*

"stringing phlox . . . grasses," de Mille, *Wings,* 25.

"strong arm" and "an hour . . . beating." Ibid., 26.

"I always . . . it." Ibid., 283.

Chapter 4

"I saw . . . 500 years." William C. de Mille, *Hollywood Saga* (New York: E. P. Dutton and Co., Inc., 1939), 58.

"village of . . . trees" Donald Hayne, ed., *The Autobiography of Cecil B. De Mille* (Englewood Cliffs, New Jersey: Prentice-Hall, Inc., 1958), 78. Uncle Cecil wrote his name using *De,* while Agnes used *de.*

"galloping tintypes" Ibid., 74.

"the graining . . . floor." de Mille, *Wings,* 199.

"The memory . . . time." de Mille, *Piper,* 87.

"dear little . . . house" Ibid., 14.

"A movie! . . . movie," and "two . . . angels," William de Mille, *Saga,* 95.

For many years the sign on the hill would read HOLLYWOODLAND to represent an early housing development.

"They hurt . . . so." Arthur Bloomfield, *San Francisco Examiner,* 8 June 1978.

"most wonderful . . . there." Agnes de Mille's diaries are located in the Dance Collection of the Performing Arts Research Center, the New York Public Library (NYPL) at Lincoln Center. Classification: MGZMD 37–1887.

Chapter 5

"we thought . . . pictures" William de Mille, *Saga,* 115.
"was throwing . . . lions" *Agnes, the Indomitable.*
"transfixed" de Mille, *Piper,* 24.
"It was . . . see." de Mille Diaries, Sunday, 6 August 1916, MGZMD 37–1386, NYPL.
"Father . . . tortures" and "it . . . around." Ibid., 18 July 1916, MGZMD 37–1386, NYPL.
"the cheers . . . animal." Ibid., November 1928, MGZMD 37–1672, NYPL.
"when they . . . tragedy." Ibid., November 1928, MGZMD 37–1672, NYPL.
"succeeded in . . . eye." Ibid., 22 March 1921, MGZMD 37–1391, NYPL.

Chapter 6

"arrange about . . . day." de Mille, *Piper,* 10.
" 'dance was . . . stage.' " Regina Woody, "How They Started," *Dance Magazine,* February 1954.
"exhibitionistic acrobatics," and "intellectual or spiritual challenge." de Mille, *Piper,* 59.
"He wanted . . . plays." de Mille, *Speak,* 8.
" 'You see . . . tennis.' " Ibid.
"Miss St. Denis . . . know." de Mille Diaries, August 1916, MGZMD 37–1387, NYPL.
"boxes, crates . . . furniture." de Mille, *Piper,* 21.
"It was . . . unreasonable," Ibid., 43.

Chapter 7

" 'no juice' " de Mille, *Piper,* 46.
"muscles were . . . unresilient" Ibid., 46.
" 'very good.' " Ibid., 52.
"ideal ballet . . . torso." Ibid., 49.
"all rusty . . . pins." Ibid.
"I sat . . . throat." Ibid., 40.
"life's work." Ibid., 47.
"Anna Pavlova . . . me," Ibid., 64.
" 'That girl . . . talent.' " Ibid., 53.

Chapter 8

"heavy, deep-bosomed . . . hipped" Ibid., 67.
"was too . . . on." Blake Green, "Agnes de Mille—Success on Her
Own, in Her Own Way," *San Francisco Chronicle,* 8 June 1978.
"I gave . . . costume," de Mille, *Piper,* 67.
"dainty and appealing" de Mille, *Speak,* 8.
"a moody . . . me.' " Ibid., 9.
"beat the . . . them." de Mille, *Piper,* 68.
" 'Pop,' " . . . college.' " Ibid., 73.
" 'All this . . . circus,' " Ibid., 77.

Chapter 9

" 'You're a . . . dancer,' " de Mille, *Piper,* 77.
"a bow . . . wires." and the spring . . . foot." de Mille Diaries, 25
June 1925, MGZMD 37–1394, NYPL.
"aching knees . . . pride." de Mille *Dance to the Piper* Manuscripts,
Agnes de Mille Collection, Sophia Smith Collection, box 6,
Smith College Archives (Smith).
"showed herself . . . footlights." *Ithaca Journal News* Scrapbooks, vol.
1, 1927–8, ZANMD2, reel 8, NYPL.

Chapter 10

" 'noncommercial.' " de Mille, *Piper,* 88.
"character studies" Ibid., 86.
" 'let the . . . do,' " Ibid., 92.
"disappointed stomach dancer," Ibid., 96.
"They sit . . . jake." Letter from Agnes de Mille to her mother,
1928, Smith.
"She leaves . . . throat." John Martin, *New York Times,* 4 March 1928.

Chapter 11

"vision" de Mille, *Piper,* 66.
" 'Long the . . . head!' " Ibid., 143.
"Ballet technique . . . possible." Ibid., 48.
"understand . . . technique" Ibid., 155.
"sustain . . . mime." Letter from Agnes de Mille to her mother, 10
January 1937, box 3, Smith.

Chapter 12

"I'm starting . . . do." Letter from Agnes de Mille to her mother, 27 November 1934, box 1, Smith.

"I'm rump-heavy . . . ankle" de Mille, *Speak*, 41.

"a good foot . . . bounce" and "sixty-four . . . pirouettes" Ibid., 10–11.

Chapter 13

"black . . . rain." de Mille, *Piper*, 188.

"London became . . . right." Letter from Agnes de Mille to her mother, 1–4 October 1938, box 3, Smith.

"stripped as at . . . repertoire." de Mille, *Piper*, 189.

" 'In a small . . . masterpiece.' " Ibid., 201.

"bounded and soared" Ibid., 204.

Chapter 14

"more opinionated . . . girl." de Mille, *Piper*, 212.

"invented time . . . movement" Agnes de Mille, "The South Bank Show," London Weekend Television, 1980, MGZIC 9–693, NYPL.

"The ballet . . . knee." Wesley Pedersen, ed. *The Dance in America.* U.S. Information Service, 1970, 71–507 (726) Smith.

" 'Thanks God, Agnes,' " de Mille, *Piper*, 227.

"If it . . . life," Ibid., 232.

"This was . . . birth." Ibid., 232.

Chapter 15

"Floor space . . . thirsty." Agnes de Mille, *And Promenade Home* (Boston: Little, Brown and Co., Atlantic Monthly Press Books, 1956), 12.

Rubbing ballet slippers in rosin keeps the dancer from slipping on the floor.

Chapter 16

"Once I'd . . . clamped." Jay Sharbutt, "Agnes de Mille, Still Going Strong." *Independent Gazette* (Berkeley), 23 December 1979.

"Nothing Agnes . . . dance," Theodore Kosloff, "Calls Agnes de Mille America's Racial Dancer," *Los Angeles Examiner,* 13 July 1930.

"exhausting process . . . simultaneously." de Mille, *Piper,* 237.

Perish forbid was an expression dance student Ruth Lert remembered hearing Agnes say in class.

"tears in his eyes." Letter from Agnes de Mille to her mother, 28 November 1942, box 3, Smith.

Chapter 17

"singable poetry." *Rodgers and Hammerstein Fact Book.* (New York: R. Rodgers and O. Hammerstein II, 1955).

"like a . . . me." de Mille, *Piper,* 247.

"I shall . . . chance." Angelica Gibbs, *New Yorker,* 14 September 1946.

"They were . . . long." de Mille, *Piper,* 254.

"peculiar . . . gift" Ibid., 256.

"conquered Broadway." George Amberg, *Ballet* (New York: New American Library, Mentor Books, 1949), 170.

"Old Master" John Martin, *New York Times,* 1 April 1942.

Chapter 18

"quaint, gay . . . daisies." Letter from Agnes de Mille to her mother, 17 June 1943, box 3, Smith.

"I've got . . . life." Ibid.

"oil . . . sidewalks," Ibid.

"simply . . . other." de Mille, *And Promenade,* 64.

" 'Do not . . . know.' " Ibid.

Chapter 21

"pretend you're . . . neck." Hilary Ostlere, "Indomitable Spirit," *Ballet News,* September 1983.

"music . . . childhood." William M. Kunstler, "Lizzie Borden— 1892 Ax Murders in Fall River, Massachusetts," *New York Times,* 13 May 1979.

"rhythm of language" *Agnes, the Indomitable.*

"name of . . . time." *The Autobiography of Cecil B. De Mille,* 41.

"You cannot . . . growing." Agnes de Mille, *To a Young Dancer*
(Boston: Little, Brown and Co., 1962).

Chapter 22

Dr. George Gorham was Agnes's doctor from New York Hospital.
While a regular X ray shows a single surface inside the body, CAT
scan X rays take many views, which are then combined to show
a three-dimensional view.
"I will" and "I can't." Agnes de Mille, *Reprieve: A Memoir* (New
York: Doubleday and Co., Inc., 1981) 69.
"small compost . . . promise" Ibid., 102, 77.
"His remark . . . eight." Ibid., 178.
"If I . . . it!" Ibid., 93.
" 'the making' " Ibid., 160.
"easily to . . . point." Ibid., 166.
"I am awake." Ibid., 204.

Chapter 23

"I wanted . . . old." de Mille, *Reprieve,* 211.
" 'You cannot . . . live.' " Ibid., 280.
"Jacobean dances . . . emotion." Julainne Konselman, "Dancers
Join Agnes for Dance History at Greek," *Valley News,* 22 June
1978. Agnes de Mille Collection, Beverly Hills Public Library.
"passion for social justice" *Agnes, the Indomitable.*
"studied war . . . poetry." Hugh Sidey, "Honoring the Unex
pected," *Time,* 28 July 1986.

Chapter 24

"She accomplished . . . stage." Walter Price, "de Mille—An American Original Returns to ABT." *Los Angeles Times,* 28 February
1988.
Agnes lost her mother in 1947; her father in 1954; her sister,
Margaret, in 1978; and her dear husband, Walter, in August
1988.

BIBLIOGRAPHY

"Agnes Surpasses Herself at the Joffrey." *San Francisco Examiner and Chronicle*, Sunday, 17 December 1978.

Amberg, George. *Ballet*. New York: New American Library, Mentor Books, 1949.

Barnes, Clive. "Agnes de Mille Is America's Moiseyev," Dance View. *New York Times*, Sunday, 17 November 1974.

Bloomfield, Arthur. *San Francisco Examiner*, 8 June 1978.

Coleman, Emily. "More of the de Mille Memoirs." *Theatre Arts*, December 1958.

Curran, Frances H. "Shakespeare and Dancing." *The American Dancer*, January 1937.

de Mille, Agnes. *America Dances*. New York: Macmillan Publishing Co., Inc., Helene Obolensky Enterprises, Inc., Books, 1980.

———. *And Promenade Home*. Boston: Little, Brown and Co., Atlantic Monthly Press Books, 1956.

———. "The Art of Ballet." *Vogue*, 1 August 1956.

———. *The Book of the Dance*. New York: Golden Press, 1963.

———. *Dance to the Piper*. Boston: Little, Brown and Co., Atlantic Monthly Press Books, 1951.

———. "Here Is America's Innocence." *New York Times Magazine*, Sunday, 30 September 1973, 15.

————. Letters and Papers. Agnes de Mille Collection, Sophia Smith Collection, Smith College Archives, Northampton, Massachusetts.

————. *Lizzie Borden—A Dance of Death.* Boston: Little, Brown and Co., Atlantic Monthly Press Books, 1968.

————. *Reprieve: A Memoir.* New York: Doubleday and Co., Inc., 1981.

————. "Russian Journals." *Dance Perspectives* 44, 1970.

————. *Speak to Me, Dance with Me.* Boston: Little, Brown and Co., Atlantic Monthly Press Books, 1973.

————. *To a Young Dancer.* Boston: Little, Brown and Co., 1962.

————. *Where the Wings Grow.* New York: Doubleday and Co., 1978.

De Mille, Cecil B. *The Autobiography of Cecil B. De Mille.* Edited by Donald Hayne. Englewood Cliffs, New Jersey: Prentice-Hall, Inc., 1958.

de Mille, William C. *Hollywood Saga.* New York: E. P. Dutton and Co., Inc., 1939.

Fonteyn, Margot. *A Dancer's World.* New York: Alfred A. Knopf, 1979.

Fowler, Carol. *Dance: Contributions of Women.* Minneapolis: Dillon Press, Inc., 1979.

Gibbs, Angelica. "Profile—Choreographer." *New Yorker,* 14 September 1946.

Graham, Martha. *San Francisco Chronicle and Examiner,* Sunday, 5 May 1985.

Green, Blake. "Agnes de Mille—Success on Her Own, in Her Own Way," *San Francisco Chronicle,* 8 June 1978.

Gruen, John. "Dance Vision," *Dance Magazine.* September 1987, 66.

Hammond, Sandra Noll. *Ballet Basics.* 2d ed. Palo Alto: Mayfield Publishing Co., 1984.

Haskell, Arnold L. *The Wonderful World of Dance.* Doubleday and Co., Inc., 1969.

Hutchinson, Ann. *Labanotation.* New York: New Directions, 1954.

Isaacson, Charles D. "Portrait as You Wait." *New York Morning Telegraph,* 17 February 1928.

Ithaca Journal News. 1927. Unnamed author. Agnes de Mille Collection. Scrapbooks, 1927–28, ZANMD2, reel 8, Dance Collection of Performing Arts Research Center, the New York Public Library at Lincoln Center.

Kerr, Walter. "Agnes de Mille: Encounter with Wisdom." *New York Times,* 5 December 1977.

Kisselgoff, Anna. "Agnes de Mille: Out of Adversity, Triumph." *New York Times,* 27 December 1976.

Konselman, Julainne. "Dancers Join Agnes for Dance History at Greek." *Valley News,* 22 June 1978. Agnes de Mille Collection, Beverly Hills Public Library.

Kosloff, Theodore. "Calls Agnes de Mille America's Racial Dancer." *Los Angeles Examiner,* 13 July 1930.

Kreuger, Miles. Interview. Institute of the American Musical, Inc., April 1988.

Kunstler, William M. "Lizzie Borden—1892 Ax Murders in Fall River, Massachusetts." *New York Times,* 13 May 1979.

———. "De Mille's Borden: How Important Is Truth?" *New York Times,* Sunday, 13 May 1979.

Lert, Ruth Clark. Interview. Ruth Clark Lert Dance Library and Archives, 17 May 1988.

Martin, John. Reviews. *New York Times,* 4 March 1928 and 1 April 1942.

"A Matter of Money—Agnes before the Senate Subcommittee." *Dance Magazine,* September 1979.

McDonagh, Don. *How to Enjoy Ballet.* New York: Doubleday and Co., Inc., 1978.

Mercer, Marilyn. "Agnes Adds New Chapter to Book." *Herald Tribune,* 20 November 1958.

Milton, Paul R. "Godchild of the Ballet." *The Dance Magazine,* June 1928, 27.

Morris, Mary. "Agnes Is Making the Name de Mille Even More Familiar." Agnes de Mille Collection, Sophia Smith Collection, Smith College Archives.

Nichols, Lewis. Review of *And Promenade Home. New York Times,* n.d.

"One Day in Pictures Was Enough for Agnes de Mille." *Boston Globe,* 30 March 1930.

Ostlere, Hilary. "Indomitable Spirit." *Ballet News,* September 1983.

Payne, Charles. *American Ballet Theatre.* New York: Alfred A. Knopf, 1977.

Pedersen, Wesley, ed. *The Dance in America.* U.S. Information Service. Smith College Library, 71–507 (726).

Perlmutter, Donna. "Agnes de Mille's Triumphant Return with Joffrey Ballet." *Los Angeles Herald Examiner,* 22 June 1978.

Price, Walter. "de Mille—An American Original Returns to ABT."
   Los Angeles Times, 28 February 1988.
Rodgers and Hammerstein Fact Book. New York: R. Rodgers and O.
   Hammerstein II, 1955.
Sharbutt, Jay. "Agnes de Mille, Still Going Strong." *Independent
   Gazette* (Berkeley), 23 December 1979.
Sidey, Hugh. "Honoring the Unexpected." *Time,* 28 July 1986.
Siegel, Marcia B. *The Shapes of Change: Images of American Dance.* Bos-
   ton: Houghton Mifflin Company, 1979.
Sorell, Walter. *Dance in Its Time.* New York: Doubleday and Co.,
   Anchor Books, 1981.
Sullivan, Robert. "Dancer Agnes de Mille Comes Up the Hard
   Way," *New York Times,* Sunday, 30 April 1944.
Werner, Vivian. *Ballet: How It All Began.* New York: Atheneum,
   1982.
Woody, Regina. "How They Started." *Dance Magazine,* February
   1954.

Video or Film

Agnes de Mille. "The Dick Cavett Show." Telecast on WNET/13,
   New York, 17 November 1977. Videotape available at Dance
   Collection of Performing Arts Research Center, the New York
   Public Library (NYPL) at Lincoln Center.
Agnes de Mille. Kennedy Center Honors interview with Dick Ca-
   vett, 22 May 1981. Videotape available at the Performing Arts
   Library, John F. Kennedy Center for the Performing Arts,
   Washington, D.C.
Agnes de Mille. "The South Bank Show." Produced and directed by
   Alan Benson, 1980. London Weekend Television. Videotape
   available at NYPL, MGZIC 9–693.
Agnes, the Indomitable de Mille. "Great Performances" on PBS. Film.
   January 1980. Videotape available at NYPL.
Conversations about the Dance. Ben Kubasik, Inc. Public Relations Ma-
   terial for Public Television. New York, 28 January 1980.
Rodgers and Hammerstein. PBS. Film. 5 February 1988 (repeat).

INDEX